Kids' Dorset

40 Family Days Out Enjoyed by Children

Sarah-Jane Forder

First published 2012 by Roving Press Ltd
This revised and updated edition published 2017

The History Press
The Mill, Brimscombe Port
Stroud, Gloucestershire, GL5 2QG
www.thehistorypress.co.uk

British Library Cataloguing in Publication Data
A catalogue record for this book is available from the
British Library.

ISBN 978 0 7509 7035 8

Typeset in Bliss
Designed by Emily Moxon
Printed in Turkey by Imak

CONTENTS

'Dorset is the PLACE to start an adventure'

JESSE

INTRODUCTION

Growing up in Dorset in the 1960s and 1970s, the outside world seemed a long way away. In those days, there were no home computers or mobile phones; watching *Blue Peter* on a rented black-and-white TV was about as hi-tech as it got. We village kids played in hedges up and down the lane, in the spinney at the top of the hill, and in Mr Peet's Patch, a wilderness beyond the garden fence. Who Mr Peet was we were never sure, but the forest of brambles and the rotting chicken house on his abandoned plot of land held an attraction. So too did the neighbouring fields where, after the harvest was in, we'd make castles and dungeons in the strawstacks.

Kids today are far more sophisticated than they ever were then, or so we generally believe. But is there anything to beat a day spent kayaking at Studland or fossiling at Lyme? Is there a child anywhere who doesn't feel the call to build a den in Thorncombe Wood or track red squirrels on Brownsea Island? Kids in Dorset are very lucky in that they have so much on their doorstep. Due to its incredible geology, the Dorset coast is now a World Heritage Site, joining the Great Barrier Reef and the Grand Canyon as one of the wonders of the natural world. It wasn't known as the Jurassic Coast when I was a child, but it was all there for the taking.

Nowadays there are many more houses and many more people: blow-ins who've come to live here as well as visitors whose stay is more fleeting. But Dorset the place – the spirit of the place – is essentially unchanged. It's still a rural landscape of countryside and coast. It's still distinctively Dorset: nowhere else in the world could possibly host the annual nettle-eating or knob-throwing championships (see page 47).

(see page 47)

The activities chosen for this book are inevitably only a selection. You'll almost certainly come across others; and be sure to keep your eyes open for the unexpected: Christmas pudding races, llama trekking and Camp Bestival are guaranteed to make memorable family days out. The annual Great Dorset Steam Fair has become a world phenomenon, and everyone knows there's nothing better than a Dorset cream tea or slice of apple cake.

Have fun, enjoy yourself, but respect the environment. Follow the Countryside Code and the Seashore Code by leaving things as you find them, and keep an eye on tides. A local saying goes: find a fossil, don't become one. Bring your sun cream and wellies, and be prepared. As one of the 11-year-old contributors to this book wisely commented, 'Dorset is unique, beautiful and unpredictable – especially the weather!'

Sarah-Jane Forder

'Getting right up close to the swans and seeing how they live was fascinating' ANNEKA

Feed the swans at the Swannery

In the 1920s the famous Russian ballerina Anna Pavlova came to Abbotsbury with her dance troupe to practise *Swan Lake* in an authentic setting. It's obvious why she bothered to make the effort. Home to the largest colony of mute swans in the UK (often more than 600 at any one time), the Swannery is at the extreme western end of the Fleet (see page 61). Eel grass, the favoured food of swans, grows in the shallow brackish water and the shoreline is fringed with reeds, a useful nesting material. Add to that the supplies of fresh water from the streams running into the Fleet, and you have the perfect gathering ground for wild swans (though called mute, they do actually snort, hiss and make grunting sounds).

They're looked after by swanherds, and have been since at least the 14th century when they were eaten as meat by the inhabitants of St Peter's Monastery in Abbotsbury (you pass the monks' historic tithe barn, now a children's play area, on your way to the Swannery). Around 150 pairs breed here, generally staying together for life and returning to the same spot each year. They build their untidy nests all over the place, even on the paths, and they don't seem to mind the large numbers of visitors. In May and June the fluffy grey cygnets hatch, and some fortunate kids will be asked to help with the mass feeding of the swans which occurs a couple of times a day.

Every two years, towards the end of July when the swans have lost their flight feathers, the birds are rounded up for monitoring. This operation involves a flotilla of canoes herding them from the Portland end of the Fleet to the Swannery bay where they are corralled overnight by a huge boom across the lagoon. Early the next day hundreds of local volunteers wade through the water to drive the swans into a holding pen so that they can be examined, weighed and measured.

The Swannery also has a real bouncing bomb (one of the Barnes Wallis prototypes that were tested on the Fleet in the early 1940s), a working duck decoy (a pond where historically wild ducks were caught for food by being lured into long netted traps) and a tall willow maze in the shape of a swan. Fast-growing willow is handy for making baskets and the Swannery reeds are still used for thatching in the village. Even today, feathers from Abbotsbury swans are sent to London to be turned into old-fashioned quill pens by Lloyd's Register of Shipping. It's therefore quite possible that the sinking of the *Titanic* in 1912 was recorded with an Abbotsbury quill.

ABBOTSBURY

🚗 DT3 4JG
OS SY576840
🅿 AMPLE FREE PARKING
👶 TOILETS WITH BABY-CHANGING FACILITIES

🚌 THE JURASSIC COAST LINK X53 RUNS REGULARLY THROUGH ABBOTSBURY

🐾 MAY NOT ENTER THE SWANNERY

🏛 THE SWANNERY CAFÉ, OPEN DAILY 10AM–4.30PM (☎ 01305 871190)

'I felt as free as a bird running down the hill. Once I'd started, I didn't want to stop.' MARTHA

Say a prayer in St Catherine's Chapel

Although set a little way back from the coast, the stone-and-thatch village of Abbotsbury was once a fishing community. Traditionally on May Day the children made garlands of flowers that were blessed in the parish church, then taken by boat and thrown into the waves as an offering to the sea. Known locally as Garland Day, the tradition still persists, although nowadays the flowery creations are placed beside Abbotsbury's war memorial safely on land.

But the village's close connection with the sea continues through St Catherine's Chapel, an imposing medieval structure built for the monks of Abbotsbury Abbey around the end of the 14th century. Perched on a hill high above the village, its isolated setting allowed the holy men to withdraw from the monastery during Lent for private prayer and meditation. It was designed to withstand the full force of the elements: the walls are over a metre thick and supported by stout buttresses, and the roof, unusually, is made of stone. That, combined with the lofty position, makes the building seem far larger than it actually is. It was able to survive the Dissolution of the Monasteries because it was an important navigational landmark for sailors. The niches in the east jamb of the south doorway reveal another of the chapel's age-old functions: one hole for the knee and two for the hands, they permit pilgrims to 'post' prayers to St Catherine asking for her help.

You can make a wish for anything you like but, St Catherine being the patron saint of spinsters, the chapel is a popular destination for women in search of a husband. The traditional prayer goes: 'A husband, St Catherine,/ A handsome one, St Catherine,/ A rich one, St Catherine,/ A nice one, St Catherine,/ And soon, St Catherine.' In a track called 'The Wind' on her 1998 album *Is This Desire?* the award-winning singer-songwriter PJ Harvey, who lives and grew up in Dorset, refers to the chapel's location on top of the hill and ends with an inversion of the above prayer, calling for a partner for the saint.

The jaw-dropping view out over Lyme Bay, with the Fleet and Chesil Beach in the foreground (see page 61), has been voted the third best in Britain by readers of *Country Life* magazine. Kids may not bother much about that, but they will love hurtling full tilt down the hill from the chapel – total exhilaration.

🚗 DT3 4JH
📍 OS SY574848
🅿 PARK AT THE SWANNERY (SEE PAGE 7) AND TAKE THE PATH UP THE HILL

🚻 PUBLIC TOILETS AT THE SWANNERY
🚌 THE JURASSIC COAST LINK X53 RUNS REGULARLY THROUGH ABBOTSBURY

🐕 WELCOME ON LEADS
☕ THE SWANNERY CAFÉ (SEE PAGE 7)

ABBOTSBURY

'The jungle bit at the bottom where all the old trees are is lush' ALFIE

Enjoy a sandwich at Mapperton

In 1762, the story goes, John Montagu, 4th Earl of Sandwich, was relaxing in a London club. A Whig politician at the height of his career, he may have been gambling or he may have been signing important papers – at any rate he needed to keep one hand free while eating. He called for meat to be served between two slices of bread, and others soon copied, asking waiters around town to 'Bring me one like Sandwich'. And so fast food was born.

All this and more you will discover at Mapperton House and Gardens, hidden deep in beautiful rolling countryside near Beaminster. Voted by readers of *Country Life* magazine as 'the nation's finest manor house', it is one of Dorset's best-kept secrets. The honey-yellow 17th-century façade, built using local sandstone from Ham Hill in Somerset, is now familiar to many as Bathsheba Everdene's farmhouse in the 2015 movie of *Far From the Madding Crowd*, starring Carey Mulligan.

The grand tour of the house includes upstairs an outrageous 16th-century pendant ceiling, the plasterwork dripping down like royal icing, and an Elizabethan bed where holes for ropes in the wooden frame beneath are clearly evident. The ropes would be pulled taut before bedtime: hence the expression 'Sleep tight'. Downstairs a portrait of Admiral Edward Montagu, 1st Earl of Sandwich and a cousin of Samuel Pepys, is a reminder that, long before the 4th Earl invented the sandwich, his great-great-grandfather was busy indulging his passion for chocolate – in the 17th century an exotic substance which was drunk, not eaten, often for medicinal purposes. The 1st Earl's 350-year-old journal contains what may be the very first recipe for chocolate ice cream, involving putting a container of liquid chocolate into a flask of snow and salt, then shaking it until it started to turn solid.

Sandwiches and Fairtrade chocolate aside (both of which are on offer in the shop and café), what kids will really go mad for are the gardens, which cascade down a green wooded valley. At the top is the croquet lawn, where you can almost imagine the Red Queen from *Alice in Wonderland*, a flamingo tucked under her arm, and on the next level an Italianate garden laid out in the 1920s with grottoes, ornamental birds and fountains. Ever descending, grassy paths draw you into the wild garden and arboretum, with low, overhanging branches to negotiate as you beat your way through like a 19th-century plant hunter. Indian runner ducks and bantams patrol the estate and you might even bump into the lord and lady of the manor, the Earl and Countess of Sandwich.

BEAMINSTER

DT8 3NR	SAWMILL CAFÉ, OPEN END
OS SY997503	OF MARCH TO END OF
	OCTOBER, DAILY EXCEPT
AMPLE CAR PARKING	SATURDAY, 11AM–5PM
WITH A PICNIC AREA	(☎ 01308 862645)
TOILETS WITH BABY-	
CHANGING FACILITIES	
ON LEADS IN THE	
CAR-PARK AREA ONLY	

'All the outfits were so inspiring it made me want to try them on' MAY

Dress for best in Blandford

The outbreak of fire was a common occurrence in Dorset towns, with their tightly packed wooden houses and thatched roofs, but this time it was different. The Great Fire of Blandford started in a tallow-chandler's house at 2pm on 4 June 1731, and quickly took hold. Within hours, most of the town had been ravaged, 74 people had died and 480 families were homeless. It was seen as a national tragedy: money poured in from well-wishers all over the country, including the king.

Two local architects, John and William Bastard, who'd already made a name for themselves, were given the job of rebuilding. The result, according to Nikolaus Pevsner, is 'one of the most satisfying Georgian ensembles anywhere in England'. For their two sisters they designed Lime Tree House, now home to Blandford Fashion Museum, a cavalcade of costumes from the 1730s to the 1970s. Here, in a series of beautifully proportioned 18th-century rooms, hot pants and mini skirts vie for attention with knickerbockers and crinolines; and the masculine shapes of the Second World War years contrast with the 'New Look' of 1947, pioneered by Christian Dior.

There's a dressing-up area for children, complete with full-length mirror, and opportunities to compare your own waist measurement with that of the ideal Victorian lady: a minuscule 45 centimetres. In Victorian England girls as young as 11 were tight-laced into corsets, and boys were dressed as girls until the age of five or six when they were 'breeched' (allowed to wear trousers). Attention is paid to accessories, too. Ladies' fans could be used to send coded messages across crowded rooms – a closed fan meaning 'I wish to speak to you', a slow fanning movement conveying 'I am married'. Thick, heavy top hats were equipped with built-in ventilators to cool the head; and in some there was a secure compartment inside the crown to conceal letters, handkerchiefs and gloves. In carrying marmalade sandwiches under his hat, Paddington Bear was following a long tradition.

Fashion, like language, is always changing. Until the 1960s, hats and gloves were regarded as essential items of clothing; and north Dorset has been a centre of glove making since the 14th century. In the mid-19th century over half the employed women in the area worked as glovers if not buttoners (see page 67). Blandford's glove factory closed down long ago, but gloves are still manufactured in Dorset by the firm of Chester Jefferies which moved to Gillingham in 1962.

(see page 67)

🚗 DT11 7AA

OS ST885064

♿ TOILETS WITH DISABLED ACCESS

🅿 PAY AND DISPLAY CAR PARK IN THE TOWN CENTRE; FREE PARKING NEAR THE RIVER

🐕 ASSISTANCE DOGS ONLY

🏛 MUSEUM TEAROOM, OPEN MONDAY, THURSDAY, FRIDAY AND SATURDAY FROM 10AM (☎ 01258 453006)

BLANDFORD

'Along the front at Bournemouth
you see loads, feel wind and
fresh air' CALLUM

Hire a beach hut in Bournemouth

The seaside resort of Bournemouth, Dorset's largest town, seems on the face of it an unlikely place for a conference of sorcerers, but it's the setting chosen by Roald Dahl for the climax of his 1983 novel *The Witches*. There, in the Hotel Magnificent, a vast white building on the seafront, the annual meeting of the 'Royal Society for the Prevention of Cruelty to Children' turns out to be a cover for something much more sinister.

Bournemouth, the narrator of *The Witches* is told by his grandmother, is full of old people who've retired there believing it will be good for their health. There is more than a little truth in this. It was a fishing hamlet and smugglers' haunt until 1810, when Lewis Tregonwell built a villa in a chine (secluded coastal valley) at the mouth of the River Bourne. Others followed, and by the late 19th century guidebooks were referring to the softness of the air, filtered through pine trees, and the mildness of the climate. The town became popular with invalids, many of them famous, including Robert Louis Stevenson who suffered from tuberculosis. While living in Bournemouth from 1884 to 1887 he completed *Kidnapped* and wrote *The Strange Case of Dr Jekyll and Mr Hyde*. Mary Shelley, author of *Frankenstein*, is buried in St Peter's churchyard, together with the heart of her poet-husband, Percy Bysshe Shelley.

The coming of the railway in 1870 brought the crowds, drawn by the miles upon miles of golden beaches, from Sandbanks in the west to Hengistbury Head in the east. Some of the UK's earliest purpose-built beach huts were erected at Bournemouth, in 1909, either side of the original pier. Among the 2,000 or so that line the town's beaches today are designer 'pods' at Boscombe Overstrand, a 'chapel' to hold weddings and civil partnerships beneath one of the historic cliff lifts, and a kids' wendy house, complete with child-size fittings, at Durley Chine.

In 2009 Bournemouth also became home to Europe's first artificial surf reef, at Boscombe. The idea was that huge sandbags on the seabed would act like a giant ramp, pushing the natural waves upwards as they crested over the top, but the design was fatally flawed. By far the best beach for families is Alum Chine, named after an unsuccessful attempt to mine and manufacture alum (a fixative used by the dyeing industry) in the 16th century. Three bridges span the narrow-sided valley, including one from which a young Winston Churchill fell while playing in 1892.

BH4 8HS
OS SZ077903
PAY AND DISPLAY CAR PARK AT ALUM CHINE

TOILETS ON SEAFRONT AT ALUM CHINE
RESTRICTED TO CERTAIN AREAS OF THE BEACH FROM MAY TO SEPTEMBER

HIRE BIKES AT BOURNEMOUTH PIER
VESUVIO RESTAURANT, OPEN DAILY FROM 10AM (01202 759100)

BOURNEMOUTH

'Crabbing always makes me feel excited. Afterwards you can sit and eat fish and chips' MEGAN

Catch a crab at West Bay

The lively market town of Bridport was founded on rope – so much so that those who ended their days hanging on the gallows were said to have been 'stabbed by a Bridport dagger'. It started in the Middle Ages when King John asked that the townsfolk made 'night and day as many ropes for ships both large and small and as many cables as you can'. His request was taken seriously. Hemp and flax were grown locally and the town's long, straight alleys were once 'rope walks' where twine and rope were laid out in lines from the backs of houses as part of a cottage industry. The town is famous for its nets too. Even today, fishing fleets all over the world use Bridport nets, and the goal nets of any major football championships are likely to have been made in Bridport, as are the tennis nets at Wimbledon.

Just over a mile from the town centre is West Bay, which used to be called, and to all intents and purposes still is, Bridport harbour (see pages 40–41). Like Weymouth, Lyme Regis, Swanage and Mudeford, it's a great place to spend a morning or afternoon crabbing, a traditional seaside activity that's surprisingly addictive. All you need is a piece of string, bait such as bacon, chicken or fish, and a weight to keep the bait on the bottom, which is where the crabs live. Wrap the line loosely round your finger and wait until you feel a crab tugging on the other end. The art is in bringing the line up with the crab still holding on – not as easy as you might think. Drop your crabs in a bucket of water with a few stones and some seaweed so they have somewhere to hide, then watch them scurry back into the water when you release them.

Round off your visit to West Bay in the adventure play area near the car park. Designed by local youngsters for kids aged 0 to 99, it has a huge sturdy boat swing and a witch's-hat climbing frame – made out of rope, it goes without saying. There are plenty of eateries in Bridport and West Bay, but don't miss the Hive Beach Café at Burton Bradstock to the east. It's renowned for its seafood, including fish caught in Lyme Bay, but it's the Lovington's ice cream and the location right on the beach that make it popular with kids. It's not a place to swim (see page 61) but to skim stones across the water, bury one another in pebbles and watch the majestic waves. Or follow the changing light and shadows on the spectacular gold-striped Burton Cliff which, in the winter of 1943, soldiers scaled as a rehearsal for the invasion of Normandy.

DT6 4EL	PUBLIC TOILETS WITH DISABLED ACCESS AND BABY-CHANGING FACILITIES AT CAR PARK AND INNER HARBOUR
OS SY462904	
PAY AND DISPLAY CAR PARK AT WEST BAY ROAD	
WELCOME ON EAST CLIFF BEACH	
THE WATCH HOUSE CAFÉ, OPEN DAILY 10AM–5PM (☎ 01308 459330)	

BRIDPORT

'I love wading through the river and climbing up trees at Cerne Abbas because it's such a secret place' JOE

Tread in the steps of the Cerne Giant

The chalk downs of Dorset present a blank canvas for large-scale art, the best-known example being the Cerne Abbas Giant (also known as the Rude Man or the Rude Giant). On the side of a steep hill above the sleepy little mid-Dorset village is carved a full-frontal, 55-metre-high figure of a naked man, the white chalk outline being created relatively easily by scouring through the thin topsoil. The grass is kept trimmed and the giant is brightened up every 25 years by its care-taker, the National Trust – most recently in 2008 when 17 tonnes of new chalk were poured on and tamped down by hand.

No one quite knows the origins of this famous landmark, so eye-catching that during the Second World War it had to be disguised to prevent its identification by enemy aircraft. Just above the giant's head is what's thought to be an Iron Age earthwork called the Trendle or Frying Pan, and possibly the chalk figure is in some way related to this. The 37-metre knobbled club and extended arm which once held a cloak certainly link it to the Greek god Heracles (Roman name Hercules), but the earliest written reference was in 1694 when the church wardens' accounts mention paying 3 shillings 'for repairing ye Giant'.

Some believe the figure was carved during the Civil War as a parody of Oliver Cromwell – Cromwell was sometimes mockingly referred to by his enemies as 'England's Hercules' – but, whenever it was made, all sorts of stories abound. One says he was a real giant who came as an invader from Denmark and was beheaded by the people of Cerne Abbas while he slept on the hillside. Other folklore, first recorded in Victorian times, associates the carving with fertility. In the past locals would erect a maypole on the Trendle, around which childless couples would dance (the site is still the scene of May Day celebrations).

Perhaps predictably, over the years the giant has been used to promote many products, including jeans, bicycles and Heineken beer – which allegedly refreshes the parts other beers cannot reach. In 2007, to the consternation of some locals, it featured in a publicity stunt for the opening of *The Simpsons Movie*. Then an oversized Homer Simpson, wielding a doughnut rather than a club, was outlined in water-based biodegradable paint just to the left of the ancient monument, which is coloured with wild flowers and butterflies in summer.

CERNE ABBAS

DT2 7AL	FREE PARKING IN A352 LAY-BY OR IN THE VILLAGE
OS ST663015	WELCOME ON LEADS
PUBLIC TOILETS IN CERNE ABBAS	THE ROYAL OAK, OPEN DAILY FROM 11AM (01300 341797)

'It's awesome jumping out
from the cracks at Corfe Castle'

JASMINE

Play hide and seek at Corfe Castle

The jagged remains of Corfe Castle topple crazily over the village of the same name, guarding the only natural route through the chalky Purbeck Hills. Although the 15-year-old Saxon king Edward the Martyr is said to have been murdered there when he went to visit his stepmother Elfrida in 978, the earliest part of the castle as we know it today was built by William the Conqueror in the 11th century. Corfe remained a royal fortress until the 16th century when Elizabeth I sold it to her lord chancellor, Sir Christopher Hatton.

The romantic ruins that now dominate the skyline are the result of Corfe Castle being blown apart with explosives by Oliver Cromwell's men during the English Civil War. Between 1642 and 1645 the castle twice came under siege by the Parliamentarians and was strongly defended by the feisty wife of the then owner, Sir John Bankes, attorney general to Charles I, who was away from home attending to the king. In the end, Brave Dame Mary, as she became known, was betrayed by one of her garrison, but the victorious Roundhead colonel was so impressed by her courage that he allowed her to take the keys of the castle when she left. They now hang in the library at nearby Kingston Lacy (see page 89) which the Bankes family built as their new home.

Quite apart from searching out the numerous hiding places and arrow slits, portcullis grooves and murder holes – gaps through which soldiers could drop rocks, hot ashes or boiling water on to the enemy – 21st-century kids can contemplate life in the dungeon of a medieval castle. Those like the one at Corfe were called *oubliettes*, from the French verb *oublier*, meaning 'to forget'. Prisoners were thrown down through a trapdoor and left to die – there were no steps to climb out. There's also a garderobe, or very basic lavatory, which focuses young minds on the wonders of modern plumbing. The slopes beneath the ramparts are ideal for rolling down.

Don't miss the Corfe Castle model village, which depicts the castle in 1646 before it was razed. Stop off too at the Ginger Pop Shop, which sells lashings of ginger beer and stocks more than 150 Enid Blyton titles. The author first visited Dorset in 1931 and holidayed in the nearby seaside resort of Swanage three times a year for more than 20 years, swimming around the piers each evening before dinner. Corfe Castle is thought to be the inspiration for Kirrin Castle in the Famous Five series. Look carefully and you may even see jackdaws flying around the towers.

BH20 5EZ
OS SY955822
CASTLE VIEW PAY AND DISPLAY CAR PARK

TOILETS WITH BABY-CHANGING FACILITIES
PARK AT NORDEN STATION AND TAKE THE STEAM TRAIN TO CORFE

WELCOME ON A LEAD
THE NATIONAL TRUST TEAROOM, OPEN DAILY 10AM–5.30PM (01929 481294)

CORFE CASTLE

CHARMOUTH BEACH

'It was quite scary being in the dock. I wouldn't want to be hanged up by the judge' TOM

Stand trial in the Old Crown Court

On 17 March 1834, six farm labourers from the village of Tolpuddle, 7 miles east of Dorchester, were brought before the London judge doing his rounds in Dorset and sentenced to seven years' hard labour in Australia. It was one of the greatest miscarriages of justice of all time, and within a few years widespread public protest caused them to be pardoned and returned to England.

The trumped-up charge of which the men were accused was making an illegal oath. In fact the Tolpuddle Martyrs, as they came to be known, had met perfectly legitimately to form a friendly society – a prototype trade union – to bargain with local landowners for better wages. Life for agricultural workers in those days was hard. Food was basic – mainly tea, bread and potatoes – and there was barely enough money for other essentials such as rent and fuel. To feed an average family, you needed 13 shillings a week, but by 1833 there was a threat of wages being reduced to only 6 shillings (about 30p in today's money).

The courtroom where the 'trial' took place remains little changed to this day. Built in the late 18th century, it was designed to intimidate. High windows behind the judge's raised dais caused light to flood down on prisoners standing in the dock. Before their hearing, they'd have spent hours if not days in the damp, dark cells beneath the building; on emerging into the glare of the court the accused would blink as their eyes adjusted, giving them a shifty, guilty look.

Modern-day visitors can sit in the dimly lit cells where prisoners awaited their fate, and then imagine the full panoply of the court being brought to bear. You can bang the judge's gavel, stand in the dock or pretend to give evidence in the witness box – said to be just far enough away from the judge's bench to prevent him being attacked with a sword. In 1815, you could be hanged for minor offences such as stealing goods worth 5 shillings (the equivalent of 25p), taking things from a shipwreck or cutting down a young tree.

Just over the way from the Old Crown Court is Judge Jeffreys restaurant, the house where in 1685 the man commonly referred to as the Hanging Judge lodged while conducting the Bloody Assizes. He earned his reputation after sentencing 200 people to death for their part in the failed Monmouth Rebellion against King James II and was said to be perpetually either drunk or in a rage. His name still resonates in Dorchester and surrounding towns and villages.

🚪 DT1 1UZ
OS SY692907
🅿 PUBLIC CAR PARKS IN CENTRAL DORCHESTER

🚻 PUBLIC TOILETS BENEATH WAITROSE (OFF SOUTH STREET)
🦮 ASSISTANCE DOGS ONLY

🍽 PREZZO, HIGH WEST STREET, OPEN DAILY 12PM–11.30PM (☎ 01305 259678)

DORCHESTER

'Hiking at Maiden Castle makes
me imagine what it was like
millions of years ago'. LUKE

Fly a kite on Maiden Castle

Along with neighbouring Hampshire and Wiltshire, Dorset has more hillforts than anywhere else in the UK: over 30 in all, ranging from smaller ones like Abbotsbury Castle in the south-west of the county to Hod Hill in the north. One of the largest, and certainly the most complex, is Maiden Castle, on the outskirts of Dorchester. The vast multiple concentric ramparts enclose an area the size of 50 football pitches, and Maiden Castle was home to several hundred people in the Iron Age (800 BC to AD 43) before the Romans took over.

The name 'castle' is somewhat confusing: there's nothing fairy tale about Maiden Castle, which is muscular and robust. The banks were made from chalk dug out of the ditches and when new would have been shiny white. Limestone walls were built to shore up the bottoms of the ramparts at the entrances, which themselves were as intricate as a maze, forcing intruders to twist through paths making them vulnerable to attack. And though the position of hillforts on the tops of hills meant they were clearly defensive, status may also have played a part.

In the 1930s, the archaeologist Sir Mortimer Wheeler unearthed an Iron Age cemetery of more than 52 skeletons on Maiden Castle. Some displayed horrific injuries such as a spearhead through the spine; others had been carefully laid in the ground with 'grave goods' – not only personal ornaments such as beads, brooches and rings but also pottery and joints of meat. At the same time, more than 20,000 sling stones – small, rounded pebbles from Chesil Beach (see page 61) – were found at one of the entrances, stored in large pits ready to be hurled at invaders.

Sheep now graze where whole communities once lived in roundhouses, going about their daily business, growing food, cooking and making textiles (view some of the finds at the Dorset County Museum, page 33). Today Dorset's hillforts make spectacular circular walks – they're high, with panoramic views, and often have plenty of wild flowers and birds. There are banks to run or roll down and wide plateaus for kite flying. Try not just Maiden Castle but also Eggardon Hill (which has an annual kite-flying festival in September), near Bridport; Lambert's Castle, near Lyme Regis; Hambledon Hill, near Blandford; and Badbury Rings, near Wimborne, where camel racing is an unexpected sport. Masters of Foxhounds from all over Dorset compete each year for a Golden Fez, which is presented to the winner on a red velvet cushion.

DT2 9PT	**AMPLE FREE PARKING**	**FINCA, GREAT WESTERN ROAD, OPEN MONDAY TO SATURDAY 9AM–4PM; SUNDAY 10AM–1PM (☎ 01305 300400)**	**DORCHESTER**
OS SY667885	PUBLIC TOILETS IN MAUMBURY ROAD WITH BABY-CHANGING FACILITIES		
WELCOME, BUT MUST BE ON LEADS WHEN SHEEP ARE GRAZING			

'I liked the medals, the dressing up and the shooting best' BEN

Do the drill at The Keep

What appears to be a Norman castle, complete with battlements and two 20-metre-high round towers, stands imposingly at the top of Dorchester. Built in 1879 as the gatehouse to the barracks of the newly formed Dorsetshire Regiment, it's now a military museum with exhibits including a prisoners' cell from the 1800s, a dazzling array of medals and – strange but true – Hitler's desk, liberated from the Führer's study in Berlin in 1945. Here you can handle rifles from the Second World War and try on original helmets, comparing the differences between German and English standard issue. There's also a laser firing range and dressing-up area for kids.

But it's the human stories that form the heart of the collection. 'Dear Jen,' wrote Private Frank Searle on a postcard to his wife in December 1914. 'Off to Wyke [Regis] tomorrow, sudden move, expect to go across the water any day now. Am in the best of health and spirits, keep up your pecker all right. Are we downhearted? No!' Four months later he was dead, killed at Ypres on the Western Front. There are touching displays of silk embroidery made not by wives and girlfriends but by soldiers in the trenches at times of respite during the fighting.

Despite the appalling conditions endured by front-line troops in France and Flanders, life in the army compared favourably with that of a Dorset farm labourer supporting a family. In 1914 agricultural wages were still low, cottages were cramped and child mortality was high. The army, on the other hand, offered job security, basic rations and accommodation, and money for drink.

Dorset's location on the south coast placed it in the firing line during the Second World War. Most of the Luftwaffe bombers passed overhead on their way to major targets such as Bristol, but from July 1940 the ports of Weymouth and Portland were attacked, as was Poole harbour. In the run-up to D-Day, whole towns and villages were taken over by American troops, and crack commando units did much of their amphibious training around Lulworth Cove (see page 39).

From The Keep battlements, there are circular views out over Dorchester and the surrounding landscape, including, in the middle distance, Poundbury Camp, an Iron Age hillfort where German prisoners were bunkered in huts during the First World War. In the opposite direction are the Borough Gardens, designed by William Goldring of Kew in 1895. The playground has equipment to suit all ages, and on warmer days there are fountains under which to run.

DORCHESTER

🅿 DT1 1RN

OS SY687906

🅿 SMALL CAR PARK
BEHIND THE MUSEUM

♿ TOILETS WITH DISABLED
ACCESS AND BABY-
CHANGING FACILITIES

🐕 ASSISTANCE DOGS ONLY

☕ THE LOFT CAFÉ,
ANTELOPE WALK,
OPEN TUESDAY
TO SATURDAY 9AM–5PM
(☎ 01305 261382)

'Feeding the animals makes me feel wonderful because they really seem to appreciate it'

ELLA

Pet the animals at Kingston Maurward

On either side of the River Frome, licking lazily along towards Wareham and Poole harbour, the land has been drained to create broad meadows and pastures: fertile, lush and green. This is prime farming territory. Thomas Hardy called it the Vale of the Great Dairies, where Tess of the d'Urbervilles worked as a milkmaid and was wooed by Angel Clare.

Just outside Dorchester, the county town, is Kingston Maurward, a large country mansion with majestic gardens and a historic landscape park. You can of course arrive by car, but far nicer is to walk over the water meadows. Leave the town on the London Road and cross over Grey's Bridge, taking care not to damage it in any way. Like several other Dorset bridges, it bears the stern warning: 'Any person wilfully injuring any part of this county bridge will be guilty of felony and upon conviction liable to be transported for life.' Go through the second gate on your right and follow the path over the fields to Three Bears Cottage (look for the bears in the thatched roof). Turn left up the narrow path to Stinsford church (where Thomas Hardy's heart is buried), then on up the hill and right to Kingston Maurward.

The big house was built in the early 18th century for the prime minister's cousin, George Pitt, and his wife Laura Grey (the family after whom Grey's Bridge is named). The original material was red brick but after derogatory comments from King George III, who was staying in nearby Weymouth, Pitt clad the exterior in Portland stone (see page 57) at enormous expense. Thomas Hardy was a frequent visitor, both as a child and later as an adult: Kingston Maurward is portrayed as Knapwater House in his novel *Desperate Remedies*.

Children will love the stone terraces, clipped topiary and winding paths through the hidden Japanese garden down by the lake, but the real winner is the animal park where you can pet goats, alpacas, rabbits and guinea pigs and enjoy activities such as cow-pat bingo, hawk talks and ferret racing. If you go in March or April you may well see a lamb being born: Kingston Maurward is not only a working farm but also a land-based college. Kids can run freely between the animals, the gardens and the playground which has a traditional wooden shepherd's hut on wheels, designed to give 24-hour shelter during lambing. Take a picnic and spend the day; just watch out for greedy goats that will quite happily snatch a paper bag of feed out of your hand and scoff the lot.

DT2 8PX

OS SY718910

TOILETS WITH BABY-CHANGING FACILITIES

AMPLE FREE PARKING

WELCOME IN THE VISITOR CENTRE BUT NOT IN THE ANIMAL PARK

THE PARK CAFÉ, OPEN DAILY 10AM–4PM (☎ 01305 215054)

DORCHESTER

'Dorset County Museum
makes me feel historic'
SAM

Eye up fossils in the County Museum

'Have you seen the museum?' asks Lucetta in Thomas Hardy's novel *The Mayor of Casterbridge*, Casterbridge being Dorchester, the town in which the book is set. 'There are crowds of interesting things: skeletons, teeth, old pots and pans, ancient boots and shoes, birds' eggs – all charmingly instructive. You'll be sure to stay till you get quite hungry.'

Hardy's novel was published in 1886, three years after the Dorset County Museum moved to its current site. It was set up to house the ancient artefacts being dug up with the building of the railway: mosaics and frescoes, jewellery and glassware made by the Romans when they founded the new town of Durnovaria around AD 70. Hardy himself had close ties with the museum, which has a reconstruction of his study from Max Gate, the house he designed and lived in just outside Dorchester for over 40 years.

In the writers' gallery of the museum, kids can dress up as Tess of the d'Urbervilles or listen to the Dorset dialect of the poet William Barnes, a teacher with progressive ideas who never used the cane. In the archaeology section, they can model as Celts or Roman soldiers, make mosaics and watch videos showing what life would have been like at Maiden Castle (see page 27). There are human remains to gape at, and even a dog skeleton with a pile of poo. Elsewhere, there's the world's first portable loo – an earth closet invented in the 19th century by the Reverend Henry Moule, vicar of Fordington in Dorchester – and a terrifying replica of the Dorset Ooser, a pagan mask in the shape of a huge wooden face with beard, wild hair, staring eyes, tombstone teeth and gigantic bull's horns upturned on either side. It's used on May Day as part of the procession of Morris dancers on top of the Giant's Hill in Cerne Abbas (see page 19).

The best bit comes at the end, in the Jurassic Coast Gallery. In 2011 Sir David Attenborough unveiled 'the world's biggest bite': the complete skull of a pliosaur, some 155 million years old, found in Weymouth Bay. About 18 metres in length and 10 metres wide, it was a top marine predator of the Jurassic period, with more powerful jaws than any other animal on earth. It rather draws your attention away from the rest of the gallery, which also has the skull of a 140-million-year-old crocodile from Swanage, dinosaur footprints cast on huge slabs of Purbeck marble, and drawer after drawer of miniature fossils that you are actually encouraged to open.

DORCHESTER

DT1 1XA
OS SY693908
TOP O' TOWN PUBLIC CAR PARK

TOILETS WITH DISABLED ACCESS AND BABY-CHANGING FACILITIES
ASSISTANCE DOGS ONLY

MUSEUM TEA ROOM, OPEN MONDAY TO SATURDAY 10AM–4PM
(☎ 01305 262735)

'I like going to Hardy's Cottage because you can play in the woods' JOSHUA

Toast crumpets in Hardy's Cottage

The picture-postcard thatched cottage on the edge of Thorncombe Wood, a few miles outside Dorchester, is where, on 2 June 1840, the great Dorset novelist and poet Thomas Hardy was born. It was a difficult birth, and the baby was thought at first to be dead until the midwife, who lived down the lane, looked more carefully and found signs of life.

The delicate infant grew into a wiry, healthy boy who walked miles each day to and from school in Dorchester and at weekends to church in nearby Stinsford (see page 31). As a child he closely observed the wildlife and people around him, and these he recorded in novels such as *Under the Greenwood Tree*, written in a little upstairs room of the cottage looking towards Black Down and its striking, 21-metre-high monument to another Thomas Hardy – the one who'll forever be associated with Lord Admiral Nelson's dying words. A distant relation of the writer, Admiral Sir Thomas Masterman Hardy lived in Portesham, near Abbotsbury (see page 9), and had a passion for local produce, especially Dorset mutton, Dorset Blue Vinny cheese and Dorset beer, which he described as 'the best ever drunk'.

Even without the literary connections, Hardy's Cottage gives a real insight into how ordinary people lived in Dorset in the 19th century. It was built in 1800 by Thomas Hardy's great-grand-father out of cob – bits of gravel, sand, chalk and clay dug out of the ground and mixed with straw and water into a kind of pudding – and for the first years of its isolated existence was used as a smugglers' store, where up to 80 barrels of brandy were hidden at a time.

Kids will marvel at the sloping floors, the low ceilings, the steep stairs – one flight like a ship's ladder – and the inglenook fireplace where, on certain days, you can put the heavy-bottomed copper kettle on to a trivet over the flames and toast crumpets using metal forks. The pretty yet productive garden is just as much fun, small gravel paths looping through crowded beds of old-fashioned lupins, lavender and roses, fruit and vegetables, with a traditional orchard beyond.

Finish your visit with a walk in Thorncombe Wood, 26 hectares of woodland and heathland grazed by wild Dartmoor ponies. In spring the wood is awash with bluebells and wild garlic, the birdsong will assault your ears and in summer you can watch dragonflies up by Rushy Pond. Bring a picnic and build a den: the perfect family day out.

DT2 8QJ | OS SY729925 | FREE PARKING AT THORNCOMBE WOOD | TOILETS AT THE VISITOR CENTRE WITH BABY-CHANGING FACILITIES | NOT ADMITTED TO THE COTTAGE | UNDER THE GREENWOOD TREE CAFÉ, OPEN DAILY 10AM–4PM (07788 851383) | DORCHESTER

'You never know what you're going to find in the rock pools at Kimmeridge' ALEX

Peer into rock pools at Kimmeridge

Once known as the Haunted Bay, Kimmeridge has an atmosphere all of its own. It's dominated by rocks, especially Kimmeridge Clay, that in the Jurassic period 155 million years ago formed the floor of a deep, tropical sea. Harder bands of limestone within the clay created a series of flat ledges that make the bay into one huge rock pool (see pages 58–59). Kimmeridge is at the centre of the Purbeck Marine Wildlife Reserve – one of the first such areas in the UK – and is a great place for snorkelling and diving as well as rock pooling and exploring.

On the site of an old fisherman's hut there's a marine centre where, in summer, you can watch the goings-on underwater via a live seabed camera. Dorset Wildlife Trust wardens run regular events including rock-pool rambles and face-only snorkelling to start you on your journey into another world – one every bit as beautiful as that on land. Parts of the seabed are hidden beneath a carpet of brittlestars, relatives of starfish, which link arms to save being swept away by the current, while others are cloaked in seagrass meadows – fields of tall grass swaying gently in the warm, shallow water. In rock pools limpets cling tightly to the sides, before at night wandering to the shore to feed on seaweed, and colourful sea anemones look more like flowers than predatory creatures waiting to catch and paralyse unsuspecting animals before swallowing them whole.

The shoreline too yields many treasures. Piles of rotting seaweed on a hot summer's day may not appeal particularly to humans – the overwhelming smell has led to part of Kimmeridge Bay becoming known as Stink Corner! – but they provide rich pickings for invertebrates which in turn are an important food source for shore birds at low tide. You may find washed-up mermaid's purses (empty egg capsules of dogfish or rays) or whelk egg cases, easily mistaken for bubble wrap. They were once used by sailors for washing, so are called sea wash balls.

Hardy plants such as rock samphire, sea rocket and sea kale grow on the cliffs, as well as uncommon species like yellow-horned poppy and wild cabbage. Visible for miles around is the Clavell Tower, where Thomas Hardy once courted the daughter of a local coastguard. It was built in 1830 as a folly, and the folly of its dramatic location became apparent as the edge of the cliff gradually advanced. In 2007 it was moved, brick by brick – all 16,272 of them – further inland and is now available as a Landmark Trust holiday let.

	KIMMERIDGE

- BH20 5PF
- OS SY909789
- P AMPLE CAR PARKING (CHARGES APPLY)
- PUBLIC TOILETS IN THE CAR PARK
- WELCOME ON THE BEACH ALL YEAR ROUND
- CLAVELL'S CAFÉ, OPEN TUESDAY TO SUNDAY 10AM–5PM (☎ 01929 480701)

'Walking in the Fossil Forest
is like walking on the moon'
NATHAN

Dawdle awhile at Durdle Door

Dorset has a propensity for strange-sounding names that kids of all ages will love: John Betjeman made play of them when he wrote of Rime Intrinsica, Fontmell Magna, Sturminster Newton and Melbury Bubb in the opening line of his famous poem about the county. Then there are the ruder monikers: Piddlehinton, Piddletrenthide, Burnt Bottom, Happy Bottom, Aunt Mary's Bottom; and, delightfully, Scratchy Bottom, a clifftop valley above Durdle Door, the spectacular limestone arch which in the early 19th century was marked on the map as Dirdale Door.

This world-famous geological feature, which made an appearance in the film *Nanny McPhee*, was formed tens of thousands of years ago by the relentless pounding of the sea. It was once part of a longer line of rocks that have since collapsed, creating a series of stumps known as the Bull, the Blind Cow and the Calf. The awesome power of the waves also sculpted the perfectly rounded bay of Lulworth Cove, to the east, painted by J.M.W. Turner in the 19th century.

Lulworth has given its name to a rare butterfly, the Lulworth skipper, and is home to another odd species, the bucket and spade tree (see it on your right just above the mill pond in West Lulworth village as you walk down to the cove from the visitor centre car park). Stair Hole, a cove in the making with its cave and blow hole, suggests what Lulworth Cove might have looked like a few hundred thousand years ago, while Man o' War Bay (see pages 76–77), just to the east of the Door, offers sheltered bathing and a reef of rocks for older kids to swim out to.

About a mile further on is the world's most complete remains of a Jurassic forest. Throughout the Jurassic period, Dorset was on the bed of a tropical sea, where clays, sandstones and limestones accumulated. Then, about 144 million years ago, sea levels dropped and a series of islands emerged, intercut with salt lagoons and channels. Soils developed and a lush forest of tall cypress and monkey puzzle trees grew alongside giant cycad ferns. When the sea rose again and covered the land, thick mats of algae spread across the forest floor. Mud deposits stuck to the algae and built up over time to form huge doughnut-shaped craters around the base of the trees.

This is the Fossil Forest that can be seen today: not a tree trunk in sight but an eerie barren landscape of rocks and stones. It runs along a wide ledge in the cliff, with the sea lashing away below, and is approached by steep steps, so is perhaps best not visited with very small children.

LULWORTH

🚗 BH20 5RN

OS SY810801

🅿 FEE-PAYING CAR PARK AT WEST LULWORTH

♿ GOOD FACILITIES AT LULWORTH HERITAGE CENTRE

👶 WELCOME ALL YEAR

🍴 THE CASTLE INN, WEST LULWORTH, OPEN DAILY 12PM–9PM (☎ 01929 400311)

WEST BAY

'I couldn't believe that so many children lived in the tiny shepherd's cottage'
ABBY

Sense the ghosts at Tyneham

In November 1943 the residents of Tyneham, a tiny village hidden deep within the folds of the Purbeck Hills, were given 28 days' notice to leave their homes as the area was being taken over by the army for use as firing ranges to train troops. The last of the displaced villagers left just before Christmas, pinning a note to the church door saying: 'Please treat our church and houses with care. We have given up our homes, where many of us have lived for generations, to help win the war to keep men free. We will return one day and thank you for treating the village kindly.'

Sadly, they were never able to come back and the buildings fell to ruin. Only the church and schoolhouse remain intact, with the children's names still on their pegs and their workbooks left open on their desks, as if they'd just run outside to play. Under the strict regime of the head-teacher, children between the ages of 5 and 14 were taught together in the one room. Talking was strictly forbidden, knuckles were rapped when the pen was held incorrectly and the Union Jack was saluted on entering school. As was common in rural Dorset, pupils were often absent at harvest time. 'Not so good an attendance this week,' notes the school diary for 16 July 1909. 'The children are kept away [to look after siblings] while the mothers carry food to the hayfields.'

In Tyneham's 'high street' – a row of four simple cottages – lived the school headteacher, Shepherd Lucas and his family of 13, labourers who worked at Tyneham Farm, and the Driscolls who ran the overbrimming general store cum post office. The Tardis-like telephone box in front must have caused quite a stir when it was first installed as most of the villagers had never seen, let alone used, such a strange contraption. All Tyneham housewives, including the rector's wife, regularly walked the dozen miles to Wareham and back for household shopping, returning with perambulators heaped with merchandise on top of babies.

After exploring the deserted houses and glades of Tyneham, go down the gwyle (pronounced goyle, an old Dorset term for a wooded glen) to Worbarrow Bay. For generations, the Miller family fished off the pebbly beach for crabs, lobsters and mackerel – sometimes as many as 6,000 in one catch. A telegram would be sent from Tyneham post office to the Wareham dealers, who would travel by horse and cart to collect the fish for market. Jutting out to sea is Worbarrow Tout, worth climbing for the intoxicating views of Brandy Bay, with its long history of smuggling.

BH20 5QF	TOILETS WITH DISABLED ACCESS AT TYNEHAM FARM
OS SY882802	
AMPLE FREE PARKING (£2 DONATION)	WELL-BEHAVED DOGS VERY WELCOME

BRING A PICNIC OR HEAD WEST TO THE CASTLE INN, WEST LULWORTH (SEE PAGE 39)	LULWORTH

'My little brother loved splashing in the puddles among the rocks, and trying to balance stones was fun.' SARAH

Walk in the Ammonite Graveyard

The 1981 film of *The French Lieutenant's Woman*, starring Meryl Streep and Jeremy Irons, has put the historic seaside resort of Lyme Regis firmly on the map. John Fowles, the author on whose novel the movie was based, lived in the town where for a number of years he worked as curator of the museum. This architectural gem is built on the site of the home of the palaeontologist Mary Anning. In 1811, at the tender age of 12, she made an extraordinary discovery on a Lyme Regis cliff-face: the world's first fossilised ichthyosaur. Mary's father, a local carpenter and cabinet-maker, had shown his children how to look for fossils and the family ran a popular curiosity shop in Lyme. Lacking a formal education, Mary taught herself to read then later went on to study geology and anatomy.

The remains of Mary Anning's ichthyosaur are now on display in London's Natural History Museum, and Lyme Regis has become a mecca for fossil hunters from across the globe. No visit there is complete without a walk in the Ammonite Graveyard on Monmouth Beach to the west of the town. On the foreshore at low tide dozens if not hundreds of giant ammonites can be seen embedded in a vast lunar landscape – actually Blue Lias rock, a type of limestone formed about 199 million years ago. Was there a mass death after mating, or maybe a local occurrence of algal bloom killed all the ammonites off? No one is quite sure.

Current geological knowledge has advanced far beyond Victorian assumptions of how the world worked. In the past ammonites were thought to be coiled snakes, or snake stones, while bullet-shaped belemnites were thunderbolts cast down from the heavens during storms. Look for real ammonites in the walls of houses and metal imitations in the lamp posts along Lyme Regis's Marine Parade. As you hunt try saying the well-known tongue-twister: 'She sells seashells on the seashore/ The shells she sells are seashells, I'm sure/ So if she sells seashells on the seashore/ Then I'm sure she sells seashore shells.' It was written in 1908 about Mary Anning, who against all odds became one of the world's leading fossil experts.

While in Lyme, keep an eye out for the natural sculptures of Adrian Gray, who balances stones haphazardly on top of one another in a way that seems to defy the laws of gravity. He's usually on Monmouth Beach at weekends and throughout the summer when the weather is fine.

LYME REGIS

🚗 DT7 3JN
OS SY335915
P MONMOUTH BEACH CAR PARK (PAY AND DISPLAY)

🚻 TOILETS WITH BABY-CHANGING FACILITIES ON THE SEAFRONT
🐾 WELCOME ALL YEAR ROUND

🍞 TOWN MILL BAKERY, COOMBE STREET, OPEN DAILY 8.30AM–4.30PM
(☎ 01297 444754)

'The Isle of Portland on the
horizon looks like a slipper'

BEE

View the world from Golden Cap

Golden Cap, the highest point on the whole of the south coast of Britain, is visible for miles around. On sunny days the reason for its name is obvious, as the orange-coloured band of sandstone catches the light and turns to burnished gold. There's a coast path leading up from Seatown, to the east, and it takes about 30 to 40 minutes to reach the top. Park at the Anchor Inn (fee), which used to be a smugglers' haunt; the cottages above were originally the coastguard station. In 1880 a whale was stranded on the stony beach and died; then after three days it began to stink to high heaven. Charles Weld, the local landowner of Chideock Manor, had the carcass cut up and disposed of – apart from the jawbones, which were cleaned and taken to the big house where they still form an arch over a wicket gate. Even if you don't encounter a whale at Seatown, you might see dolphins feeding on shoals of mackerel in the tiny cove.

The less strenuous way up Golden Cap is to walk from the National Trust's Langdon Wood, through Corsican pines that with the blue sea beyond give a Mediterranean feel. At the summit, take in the sweeping views towards Portland Bill to the east and Start Point (in neighbouring Devon) to the west. Down below is the deserted village of Stanton St Gabriel where 26 families used to live. The coming of the main road in the 18th century caused the villagers to drift away, and only a ruined farmhouse and 13th-century chapel now remain. From here, down some very steep steps, is St Gabriel's Beach, so secluded you're likely to have the place to yourself. Back in the car park at Langdon Wood, there's an adventure play trail where kids can swing like chimps off chains and ropes.

Before you head off, pay a visit to Moores Biscuit Factory in Morcombelake. The family started baking biscuits here in 1880, the most famous being the Dorset Knob, a small, hard, round bread roll originally cooked overnight in the dying heat of a wood-fired oven. They were once a staple of farming folk who poured hot tea over them and ate them for breakfast, but are now usually enjoyed with cheese, especially Dorset Blue Vinny (see page 75). The village of Cattistock, to the north-east, holds an annual Dorset Knob Throwing Contest, which includes fixtures such as knob eating, knob painting, knob and spoon races, knob darts and guess the weight of the big knob. Cattistock is home to a famous hunt and the baying of hounds can sometimes be heard.

🚶 DT6 6EP
OS SY407923
🅿 LANGDON HILL CAR PARK (FREE FOR NT MEMBERS)

🚻 PUBLIC TOILETS BY THE NATIONAL TRUST SHOP, STONEBARROW HILL
🐾 WELCOME ALL YEAR

🍴 THE ANCHOR INN, SEATOWN, OPEN DAILY 10AM–11PM (☎ 01297 489215)

MORCOMBELAKE

'You can stay at Moreton for hours, chasing tiny fish through the still clear water' MILLIE

Ford the River Frome at Moreton

Salmon and brown trout slip by unnoticed along the River Frome, but at the picturesque village ford in Moreton – said to be the widest such crossing in the south of England – it's the tiddlers that local children come to catch, armed with fishing nets, buckets and jam-jars. On boiling days it's a great place to cool down, with shallows no more than a few inches deep shaded by over-hanging trees. There's a rope swing on one of the banks, and a long, narrow bridge for those who prefer to keep feet firmly on dry land. Rare water voles and otters live on the Frome; kingfishers too. Visit early or late in the day and you may catch a fleeting glimpse of one.

The track beyond leads through Moreton Plantation and emerges near Clouds Hill, former home of the soldier, writer and historian T.E. Lawrence – better known as Lawrence of Arabia. Famed for his role in the Middle Eastern campaign of the First World War, he sought privacy in a small estate-worker's cottage enveloped by trees. While stationed at nearby Bovington Camp (see page 93), he spent most of his time at Clouds Hill reading, writing and listening to music. He had no need of luxuries – the cottage had no mains electricity and no loo – and lived on picnic meals washed down with China tea. He never drank alcohol and always ate standing up at the wide mantelpiece deliberately set at a convenient height.

The cottage that you see today is pretty much as Lawrence left it. The upstairs music room, like a modern loft studio complete with prototype Velux window, is flooded with natural light and dominated by an enormous wind-up gramophone. A smaller, darker room along the landing has a homemade ship's bunk, a porthole window and walls covered with aluminium foil for insulation. Downstairs the walls of the main room are lined with books, and most of the available space is filled with a vast square leather divan. Lawrence used it as a sofa during the day and converted it to a bed at night simply by rolling out his sleeping bag.

Apart from books and music, Lawrence's other great passion was motorbikes. Sadly, in May 1935, he died after crashing at 90 mph on the way back from Bovington; he is buried in the graveyard at Moreton. Every year thousands of people come to see his headstone, as well as the famous clear-glass windows engraved in the nearby church by Laurence Whistler after a bomb destroyed all the existing stained glass in 1940.

DT2 8RJ
OS SY806895
TOILETS WITH BABY-CHANGING FACILITIES AT THE TEAROOMS

PARK ON THE ROADSIDE IN THE VILLAGE
WELCOME AT THE TEAROOMS BUT NOT INSIDE CLOUDS HILL

MORETON TEAROOMS, OPEN DAILY MAY TO SEPTEMBER, 10AM–5PM (☎ 01929 463647)

MORETON

POOLE POTTERY

FREYA

'My best bit was designing the pottery tiles. My worst bit was the scary dentist's chair' GEMMA

Live the maritime life in Poole

Poole is inextricably linked with the sea. It's all there in the coat of arms: the wavy bars of black and gold representing the ocean, the leaping dolphin and the scallop shells – the last referring to the shrine of St James at Santiago de Compostela visited by pilgrims leaving Poole in the Middle Ages. The town has one of the largest natural harbours in the world, covering more than 4,000 hectares: three times the size of Lake Windermere. The shallow water, mudflats and saltmarshes attract huge numbers of birds – up to 20,000 in the winter – and it's in an Area of Outstanding Natural Beauty. Yet beneath all this lies Britain's largest onshore oilfield, operated by BP from Wytch Farm on the harbour's southern shores. Look carefully and you may just make out a few 'nodding donkeys' (the constantly moving pumping units).

Remains of two Iron Age jetties from about 250 BC have been discovered in the harbour, and Poole may well be Britain's oldest cross-Channel port. Wool from the backs of Dorset sheep was shipped to France and Flanders in the 13th century, but the town's golden age was based on cod. In the 17th and 18th centuries, ships sailed to Newfoundland loaded with men and provisions, brought salt fish back to the Mediterranean countries of southern Europe and finally returned home bringing wine, olive oil and dried fruits.

The notorious 15th-century pirate Harry Paye operated from one of the small islands in Poole harbour. Described as 'a knight who scours the seas', he was feared by the French and Spanish who called him 'Arripay'. In 1407 his ships captured 120 merchant vessels in the English Channel carrying vast quantities of the best French wine. Tradition has it that the townsfolk of Poole celebrated by eating, drinking and making merry for weeks. Three centuries later another Poole adventurer, Captain Woodes Rogers, rescued from an island in the South Pacific the marooned sailor Alexander Selkirk who became the model for Daniel Defoe's Robinson Crusoe.

The story of all this and more is told in the glass-fronted Poole Museum based in a 19th-century warehouse near the historic old quay. Highlights include the stunning Iron Age logboat, the largest ever found in southern Britain, and a complete display of Poole Pottery. From the terrace at the top of the museum you can see right out over the harbour, where you may catch sight of a sleek, locally made Sunseeker yacht like the ones used in James Bond films.

POOLE

⌂ BH15 1SB	⊞ TOILETS WITH DISABLED ACCESS AND BABY-CHANGING FACILITIES
OS SY008903	
P QUAY VISITORS' CAR PARK (PAY AND DISPLAY)	✻ ASSISTANCE DOGS ONLY

☕ CAFÉ EXPLORE, OPEN MONDAY TO SATURDAY 10AM–5PM; SUNDAY 12PM–5PM (☎ 01202 262615)

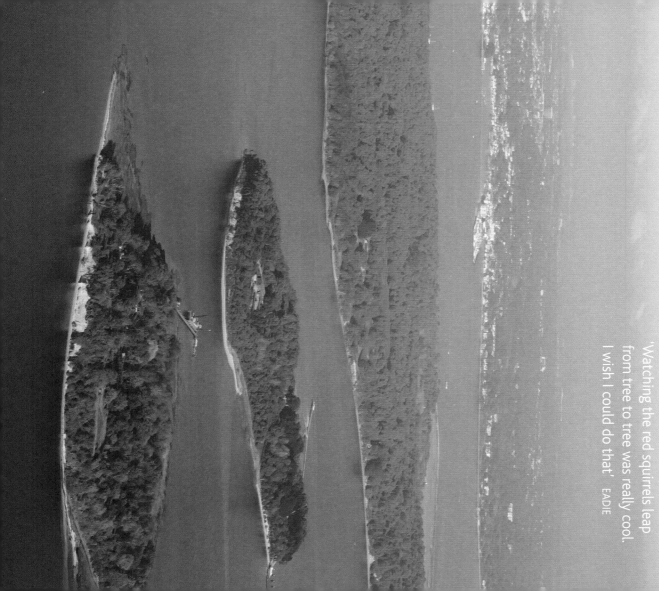

'Watching the red squirrels leap
from tree to tree was really cool.
I wish I could do that' EADIE

Hop on a ferry to Brownsea Island

In 1956 a local lad, aged eight, visited Brownsea Island, the largest of five main islands in Poole harbour (see page 51). 'We went to tea at the castle,' he recalled, 'and started with a fruit salad, which had been prepared days earlier and was covered with dust and dead insects. This was then followed by a salad with brown-edged lettuce leaves and curled-up stale bread and butter. There was a deer in the kitchen, curtains in shreds, windows broken and live rats and mice on the table. Mrs Bonham-Christie had the audacity to admonish me for not using my side plate correctly.'

This was perhaps typical eccentricity on the part of the last private owner of Brownsea, a recluse who forbade the killing of any animal on the island, including worms dug for bait, and refused to allow anyone to land. But that was nothing compared with previous incumbents: one was called 'Mad' Benson and is said to have dabbled in black magic, another committed suicide, and a third bankrupted himself in a doomed attempt to manufacture pottery. Brownsea is now known primarily as the birthplace of the Scouting movement, started by Robert Baden-Powell in August 1907. At the first camp 22 boys were woken by a shrill blast on an African horn, followed by cocoa, exercises, flag break and prayers before the day's activities of stalking, tracking, building shelters and racing in boats.

Thought to be the inspiration for Enid Blyton's Whispering Island in the Famous Five books, Brownsea Island is still a child's paradise. Not only is there the thrill of arriving by boat, but there are secret beaches to discover, trees to climb, fields to horse about in, and peacocks strutting around as if they own the joint. Most of all, it's the best place for seeing wildlife in Dorset. So said Bill Oddie when Brownsea hosted the BBC's *Autumnwatch* in 2008.

Autumn – the nut-gathering season – is the optimum time of year to see red squirrels: tiny creatures half the size of a grey, and one of the UK's most endangered species. There are between 100 and 200 of them living on Brownsea, which with the handful of other small islands in Poole harbour and the Isle of Wight is the only place in southern England where they survive. They can be found in most wooded parts of the island – which amounts to the majority of it – but you have a better chance of spotting one in the morning or late afternoon and if you look upwards (they spend most of their time in trees). It'll be an encounter you and your kids will never forget.

BH13 7EE	VILLANO CAFÉ,
OS SZ010873	OPEN DAILY MARCH TO
PARK AT POOLE QUAY OR	OCTOBER 10AM–5PM
SANDBANKS FOR FERRY	(☎ 01202 707744)
LINKS TO THE ISLAND	
TOILETS WITH DISABLED	
ACCESS AND BABY-	
CHANGING FACILITIES	
NOT PERMITTED ON	
THE ISLAND	

POOLE

'It was so much fun trying on the armour and pretending to load and fire the guns' NICKY

Commandeer a castle on Portland

The larger-than-life figure of Henry VIII greets you in the great hall of Portland Castle, one of a series of coastal fortresses built by the king in the 16th century to protect England from the threat of invasion by France and Spain. Overlooking Portland harbour – the deepest artificial one in the UK – naturally the castle is made of local Portland stone (see page 57). The harbour's massive breakwaters are of the same material, quarried by convict labour in the 19th century.

In Tudor times the castle was state of the art, equipped with the most up-to-date weapons and squatting solidly just above sea level so that cannon could fire straight at enemy ships. As it turned out, the fortifications were never tested but, together with its twin at Sandsfoot, a couple of miles away on the other side of the harbour, Portland Castle acted as a formidable deterrent. In the 18th and early 19th centuries it was used by the authorities as a lookout for smugglers and during the Second World War it played an important part in preparations for D-Day.

Portland Castle's modest proportions make it ideal for kids, who can try on 17th-century breastplates and helmets in the armoury and handle reproduction gunners' tools in the gun room. Enjoy the sea views from the upper gun platform and relax afterwards in the Governor's Garden, with its impressive circular amphitheatre made from Portland stone. There's a free, mostly child-friendly audio guide to the castle and a series of family events throughout the year.

Follow your history lesson with a trip to Church Ope Cove ('ope' means 'opening' in an other-wise impenetrable coastal landscape). Though it's a steep climb to get there and the beach is stony not sandy, it's well worth the effort. Backed by a shambles of wooden sheds with pretty stone gardens, it's long been a favourite with locals for swimming and launching boats. On your way back up, go by the ruined church of St Andrew and its 'pirate' graves. The skull and crossbones is a Masonic emblem as well as a symbol of death, so there is lots of room for the imagination.

At the tip of the island, which is not really an island at all as it's linked to the mainland by Chesil Beach (see page 61), is Portland Bill. Check out the three lighthouses, built to warn shipping to steer well clear of the deadly currents of Portland Race. Pulpit Rock, a huge stack jabbing out into the sea, was formed as a result of quarrying in 1875. If you're feeling brave, stand with your back against it and feel the waves pounding away beneath you.

PORTLAND

DT5 1AZ

OS SY685744

P FREE CAR PARK CLOSE TO THE FRONT ENTRANCE

TOILETS WITH DISABLED ACCESS AND BABY-CHANGING FACILITIES

WELCOME ON LEADS IN THE GROUNDS

THE CAPTAIN'S TEAROOM, OPEN DAILY 11AM–4PM (☎ 01305 820539)

'There were so many sculptures to hunt for; my favourite was the stone bear whose nose was smooth enough to stroke' SUSIE

Rock on in Tout Quarry

Portland is famous the world over for its creamy-white stone, used in iconic buildings such as St Paul's Cathedral, Buckingham Palace and the British Museum in London as well as the United Nations headquarters in New York. Architects and stone masons favour it because though hard-wearing and weather resistant it can be easily cut and carved. Tout Quarry at the top of Portland ('tout' is dialect for lookout point) was last worked about 90 years ago; before that it was a scene of much activity, with quarrymen hewing the heavy stone blocks and moving them by quarry jack, crane and railway to be shipped around Britain and abroad. Since then wildlife has taken over: once a site of industry, the quarry is now a protected Site of Special Scientific Interest. Bee and pyramidal orchids can be seen during the summer months; some plants are so rare they are only found on Portland.

Sculptors have taken over too: in Tout there are around 100 three-dimensional artworks, either carved into the rock face itself, made from shale or worked from the post-industrial landscape. The entrance is fairly unprepossessing, but you soon find yourself in a labyrinth of deep rock gullies smothered in vegetation. Here, since the 1980s, mermaids, mammoths, flying books and hearths have been conjured out of stone by artists and students from all over the planet. The first to work in Tout was the internationally known sculptor Antony Gormley, who won the Turner Prize in 1994: look for his *Still Falling*, a lifesize figure frozen in mid-dive. You have to hunt to find the sculptures, sometimes clambering up and under boulders to seek them out, and don't miss either the old quarrymen's shelter gouged out of the rock behind Lano's Arch. One of several manmade caves used in the past for meal breaks and during bad weather, it's an atmospheric place for a picnic on a rainy day.

A word to the wise: at Tout Quarry you will see plenty of evidence of them, but do not under any circumstances on Portland say the word 'rabbits'; use instead 'bunnies', 'underground mutton' or 'long-eared furry things'. Local quarrymen have been known to refuse to go to work when they see rabbits, believing that they cause landslides. When the Wallace and Gromit film *The Curse of the Were-Rabbit* came out in 2005, special posters had to be made for Portland, changing the title to the more acceptable *Something Bunny is Going On.*

PORTLAND

🅿 DT5 2LN	🏨 HEIGHTS HOTEL BISTRO
OS SY686726	AND COFFEE SHOP,
🅿 FREE CAR PARK	OPEN DAILY FROM 7.30AM
	(☎ 01305 821361)
🚻 PUBLIC TOILETS BEHIND	
THE HEIGHTS HOTEL	
🐾 MOST WELCOME	

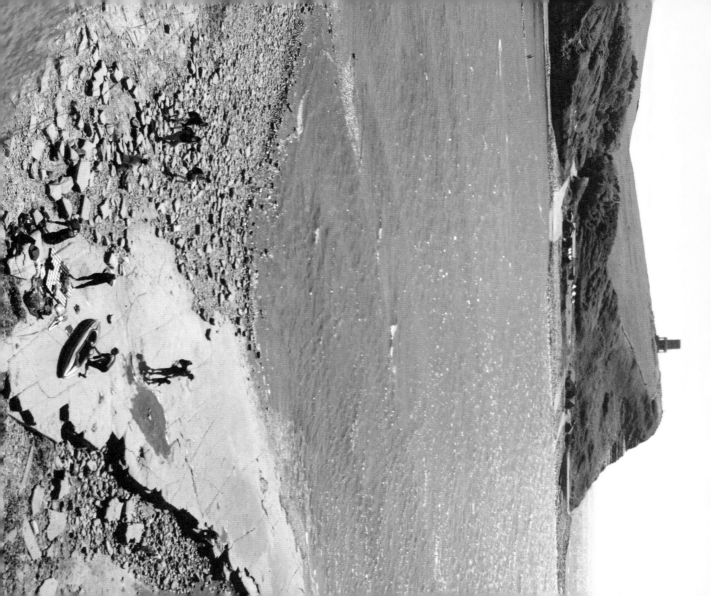

KIMMERIDGE

'Fishing on Chesil Beach makes me feel weightless and happy, like I'm in a dream' OLIVER

Fish for your supper on Chesil Beach

Forget all notions of sand between your toes when you come to Chesil Beach, known properly as Chesil Bank. An accumulation of 100 million tonnes of pebbles that can be seen from space, it runs for about 18 miles between West Bay and Portland. In places it's up to 15 metres high and 200 metres across, and the pebbles too vary greatly in size. The largest, at Portland, are called cobbles and are as big as saucers, while the smallest, at West Bay, are about the size of peas. This grading, caused by the action of the westerly waves hitting the bank at an angle, pushing the shingle along to the south-east, has proved a blessing for local fishermen and smugglers landing in fog or at night. They could tell exactly where they were just by the size of the stones.

Chesil is no place to swim – it shelves away sharply and the undertow is lethal – but is popular for fishing: at Cogden, West Bexington and Abbotsbury as well as Ferrybridge (see below). In late spring and early summer mackerel shoal in large numbers along the length of the beach, but almost any fish that swims in UK waters can be caught off Chesil. If you're lucky you may even see a lerret, a wooden boat designed in 1615 specially for launching from and landing on the steep bank. Though primarily used for mackerel fishing, in the 1830s the newly formed RNLI put two lerrets into service as lifeboats. Not before time: the Portland end of Chesil Bank is nicknamed Deadman's Bay because so many ships have been wrecked there over the years. On stormy nights, when the back-suck of the pebbles can be heard for miles inland, it's easy to empathise with the 15-year-old hero of John Meade Falkner's Victorian smuggling adventure *Moonfleet*: "Tis then I turn in bed and thank God ... that I am not fighting for my life on Moonfleet Beach.'

The still waters of the Fleet, protected behind the natural barrier of Chesil Bank, couldn't be more of a contrast. The largest lagoon in England, a combination of fresh, salt and brackish water, it's 8 miles long and the size of 600 football pitches. Like Chesil, it is important for its wildlife. While Chesil has nesting little terns – one of the UK's rarest seabirds – the Fleet has more than 150 different types of seaweed, 25 species of fish and 60 species of mollusc. Thousands of brent geese from Siberia and wigeon from Russia spend the winter there feeding plentifully. An underwater camera relays real-time footage back to the Chesil Beach Centre, or you can take a trip round the Fleet on an observatory boat which leaves from Ferrybridge at the start of the causeway.

DT4 9XE
SY668756
PUBLIC CAR PARK BESIDE THE VISITOR CENTRE

TOILETS WITH BABY-CHANGING FACILITIES
WELCOME IN THE VISITOR CENTRE

TASTE CAFÉ, CHESIL BEACH CENTRE, OPEN DAILY FROM 10AM (☎ 01305 206191)

PORTLAND

'Verwood's great because you don't really get a chance to see heavy horses anywhere else'

REBECCA

Groom a heavy horse at Verwood

Wherever you go in Dorset, you'll see horses: in fields and paddocks, grazing on verges, even being ridden along quiet roads. It's a constant reminder of the county's rural roots. Unless you go to Verwood, though, you're unlikely to see heavy horses. They are a dying breed.

The medieval great horse came to England with William the Conqueror in 1066. It was bred to be strong enough to carry an armoured knight complete with cumbersome weapons, yet still have the agility to move out of danger or in for the kill during battle. Later its strength was put to use doing hard work on the land: pulling carts and ploughing the soil. Before the development of the internal combustion engine, heavy horses were vital to the country's economy.

Although heavies were harnessed once again during the First and Second World Wars, as depicted in Michael Morpurgo's novel, play and film *War Horse*, increased mechanisation in the 20th century saw their gradual decline. The Heavy Horse Centre at Verwood, which also has a colourful display of horse-drawn gypsy wagons, is doing its best to halt that trend.

Gypsies, who originally came from India, in fact had little time for heavy horses, preferring to use Welsh cob ponies to pull their caravans. Cobs are sturdy, cheaper to feed and shoe than heavy breeds, have fewer medical problems and generally live longer. Here you can find out all about this as well as feed and groom the horses and learn how to harness them. You can mount a pony, take a ride in a wagon drawn by one of the heavies, or enjoy a spin in a doll's-size trap powered by a miniature Shetland. You can also drive a tractor.

There's a real gypsy caravan in the children's playground, as well as a travelling showman's wagon to look around in one of the sheds. The amount of gold paint on the sides reflected a person's status – much as the amount of chrome on modern motor-pulled gypsy caravans is a symbol of wealth. The space inside was only for sleeping in; every other part of life took place outside. Sadly, like the heavy horses, the traditional wagons are becoming extinct; the few that remain are now collectors' pieces.

If you happen to see a gypsy caravan and ponies anywhere in the Dorset countryside, it might strike you as idyllic. But there is little romance in being on the road nowadays: only a dogged determination to maintain a culture and an ancient way of life.

BH21 5RJ
os SU085113
P AMPLE FREE PARKING

B TOILETS WITH DISABLED ACCESS AND BABY-CHANGING FACILITIES
' WELCOME ON LEADS

B SMOKEY JOE'S RANCH CAFÉ, OPEN TUESDAY TO SUNDAY MARCH TO OCTOBER, 10AM–4PM (☎ 01202 824040)

RINGWOOD

'Being in the forest makes
you feel better'   RYAN

Cycle through the forest at Moors Valley

Traffic hurtles along the A31 outside Ringwood, seemingly oblivious to what lies just beyond. The clue's in the name of the nearby towns: Ringwood certainly, but also Verwood, originally recorded in 1288 as Beau Bois (French for beautiful wood). For hundreds of years it was known as Fairwood until, over time, the burring Dorset vernacular changed it to Verwood. Where there was once a wild and desolate heath, whose rich clay seams and plentiful brushwood fired a traditional pottery industry, there is now hectare after hectare of planted pine trees, as far as the eye can see. By no stretch of the imagination is Ringwood Forest anything like the New Forest, just over the border in Hampshire, but it has its own magic, not least its capacity to soak up vast numbers of visitors. It's the Forestry Commission's most popular site in the UK.

One of the main points of entry to the forest is through Moors Valley Country Park, owned by East Dorset District Council. From here you can walk or cycle round a choice of waymarked trails, either wide, level gravel tracks or undulating, narrow paths that slalom through the trees. None of which seems to deter the wildlife. Early in the morning you may catch a glimpse of a shy roe deer, you might see dragonflies hovering over the park's many lakes in the midday sun, or hear nightjars churring as dusk falls. Adders and other reptiles live in the forest, as do at least four different species of bats and more than 100 species of moths.

There's a permanent orienteering course with 50 markers as well as a 2-mile fitness trail, with benches, parallel bars, beams and hurdles offering exercises for different muscle groups and varying abilities. A giant ants' nest, a snake pit and an enormous spider's web, all made from timber and rope, are part of a mile-long trail to entice families with small children away from the playgrounds, steam train and central lake, and into the deep, dark wood. Sections of the route take you ducking under overhanging branches, while above your head whizz older children and adults enjoying Go Ape, a high-wire assault course of zip lines, Tarzan swings and rope ladders for adrenalin junkies.

If hurling yourself from the treetops seems a bit much, you can still get a great aerial view of the forest from an elevated walkway 5 metres above ground level. Stand on the wooden platform, close your eyes, inhale the smell of pine and listen to the wind whispering through the trees.

RINGWOOD

⚓ BH24 2ET
OS SU115062
🅿 AMPLE PARKING (PAY AS YOU LEAVE)

🚻 TOILETS WITH DISABLED ACCESS AND BABY-CHANGING FACILITIES
🐾 WELCOME ON LEADS

🍴 SEASONS RESTAURANT, OPEN DAILY 9AM–5PM (☎ 01425 470537)

'The best things in the museum are the old-fashioned typewriter and the mummified cat' JENNIFER

Star in an ad on Gold Hill

It's been voted the favourite ad of all time. A small boy pushes a bike laden with loaves of bread up a steep cobbled street to the strains of Dvořák's 'New World' symphony. It appears to be somewhere in the north of England. But the 1973 Hovis commercial, directed by Ridley Scott who went on to make Hollywood blockbusters such as *Alien* and *Gladiator*, was actually filmed on Gold Hill in Shaftesbury, which at 200 metres above sea level is Dorset's highest town.

Gold Hill is a corruption of Guild Hill, a reference to the craftsmen who sold their wares to pilgrims visiting the abbey where the bones of Edward the Martyr had been laid to rest in 978. By the 14th century, the abbey had become the richest Benedictine nunnery in the country and Shaftesbury the most populous place in Dorset. There were 12 medieval churches and at least as many inns: Thomas Hardy claimed that in Shaftesbury beer was more plentiful than water.

The town overlooks the Blackmore Vale, and some of the best views are to be had from the pretty walled garden of the Gold Hill Museum, once a hostel providing overnight accommodation for drovers, jugglers and traders attending Shaftesbury's markets and fairs. The star exhibit is the Byzant, an exotic object of gilded wood which would be ritually presented every year to the Lord of the Manor of Gillingham, with gifts of ale, bread, a calf's head and gloves. The purpose was to confirm the town's right to water from a spring outside its boundaries.

Elsewhere in the museum Dorset's oldest fire engine rubs shoulders with a mummified cat found in a local cottage roof (dead cats, chickens or old shoes were often left in house spaces by 17th-century builders for good luck), a working Remington typewriter, a heavy Bakelite telephone that you can dial and a serpent (an S-shaped brass instrument related to the modern tuba).

Plenty of space is devoted to Dorset's button-making industry, which took off in Shaftesbury in 1622. By 1658 there were 31 different button designs, including the High Top and the Dorset Knob (the famous Dorset Knob biscuit, see page 47, is probably named after the button due to its similarity in shape). The buttons were in high demand: by the end of the 18th century about 4,000 women and children from outlying villages were churning them out. But in 1851, when a button-making machine was shown at London's Great Exhibition, it was curtains for Dorset's cottage industry. Many who'd depended on it for their livelihood were forced to emigrate.

SHAFTESBURY

🏠 SP7 8JW
OS ST863229
🅿 PUBLIC CAR PARKS IN THE TOWN CENTRE

♿ TOILETS WITH DISABLED ACCESS AND BABY-CHANGING FACILITIES
🦮 ASSISTANCE DOGS ONLY

🏛 THE SALT CELLAR, OPEN MONDAY TO SATURDAY 9AM–5PM (☎ 01747 851838)

'My favourite place is the old castle because you can hide in the ruins and think what it was like in the olden days'. ELLIE

Romance the stones in Sherborne

Sir Walter Raleigh – the dashing poet and adventurer who may or may not have spread his cloak over a puddle for Queen Elizabeth I and who's reputed to have introduced potatoes and tobacco to the English court from the Americas – is better known for his foreign travels than his home-making abilities. But when he first caught sight of the 12th-century Sherborne Old Castle, he decided he must have it. In 1592, with the help of Queen Elizabeth, he initially leased and then purchased the decaying building before starting the process of modernisation.

He soon got bored with the project, and money ran out, so within two years of acquiring the estate he began building a new home which he called Sherborne Lodge. That rectangular, four-storey house is now confusingly known as Sherborne Castle and you can see it through the trees from the old castle – the proper castle – which is the place for kids. The original structure was blitzed by Parliamentary forces during the English Civil War, and what greets you today is a crumbling cascade of arched doorways and cutaway walls with glimpses of the sky beyond. It is a castle of the imagination: don't be surprised to see sword-waving children running across the bridge to the gatehouse or mock-fighting in the dry moat down below.

The two are no longer interconnected – you have to travel by road between their respective entrances – but when the young (and then unknown) Capability Brown landscaped the grounds in the 18th century the romantic silhouette of the old castle became a backdrop to the lake put in to enhance the views from the new house. In the gardens of the later building you can still see the stone seat where, so it's said, one evening Raleigh was enjoying a quiet smoke when he was suddenly dowsed with ale by an anxious servant believing his master was on fire.

If touring Sherborne Castle with younger adventurers, get them to look for the pipe allegedly presented to Raleigh by American Indians, the super-sized bath tap, the 19th-century man trap for catching poachers and the set of false teeth belonging to Lord Digby, ancestor of the current owner. Or see how many ostriches they can spot – an ostrich with a horseshoe in its beak being the Digby family crest. These exotic birds can be found all over the place: adorning the ceiling plasterwork, supporting tables, sculpted into chandeliers and painted on to porcelain cups and saucers. Symbolically, the ostrich signifies watchfulness and strength.

SHERBORNE

DT9 3SA

OS ST648168

FREE CAR PARK AT THE OLD CASTLE

TOILET WITH DISABLED ACCESS

WELCOME ON LEADS

THE WALLED GARDEN RESTAURANT, OPEN DAILY 10AM–4.30PM (☎ 01935 814345)

'The water at Studland is warm and shallow and good for kayaks' STELLA

Leap among the dunes at Studland

The ancient village of Studland was the inspiration for Toytown in Enid Blyton's *Noddy* (see page 21), but it's the beaches round the curving bay that most people come to enjoy. The 4-mile stretch of golden sand shelves gently into the sea and at Knoll Beach, which is the hub, you can hire kayaks and pedaloes – even a beach hut for the day or week if that takes your fancy. In high summer a big attraction for children is the ice-cream boat that cruises along selling drinks and lollies at premium prices. Seahorses have been discovered in the bay, where they live among the beds of eel grass, and there is so much else to explore.

The beaches are backed by sand dunes and heathland of the type vividly brought to life by Thomas Hardy in *The Return of the Native*. This rare habitat, part of a National Nature Reserve, is home to all six native British reptiles: smooth snake, sand lizard, common lizard, slow worm, grass snake and adder (see page 81). You may see stonechats on top of the yellow gorse bushes, their call resembling the sound of pebbles being banged together. You may be really lucky and spot a roe or sika deer: dawn and dusk are the best times. Bird hides surround a shimmering lake called Little Sea, which was open to the ocean until around 1880 when the developing sand dunes cut it off: it's a good place to watch little egrets wading around looking for food. Brooding above a low knoll is the Agglestone, a great hulk of sandstone some 5 metres high, 24 metres in circumference and weighing in at around 400 tonnes. According to local doggerel, it was 'said to be by Satan thrown/ at Corfe Castle in the night/ from the neighbouring Isle of Wight'.

Studland is also rich in history, having been used as a training area during the preparations for D-Day in the Second World War. Look out for pillboxes and anti-tank devices called dragon's teeth, and at Middle Beach the concrete observation bunker called Fort Henry, where King George VI, Churchill, Montgomery and Eisenhower met in April 1944 to discuss the coming battle.

Rising out of the sea are the white chalk stacks of Old Harry Rocks, Old Harry being a popular term for the Devil. Or perhaps they were named after Harry Paye, a 15th-century pirate who regularly attacked merchant ships leaving Poole harbour (see page 51). At any rate, Old Harry's Wife, a smaller stack, collapsed in 1896, though Old Harry's Daughter lives on. In the cliffs are caves called the Devil's Den, which are always warm – the fires of Hell have left their mark there.

BH19 3AQ

OS SZ034835

P KNOLL BEACH CAR PARK (FREE TO NT MEMBERS)

♿ TOILETS WITH DISABLED ACCESS AND BABY-CHANGING FACILITIES

WELCOME BUT RESTRICTIONS APPLY

KNOLL BEACH CAFÉ, OPEN DAILY 10AM–4PM (☎ 01929 450305)

STUDLAND

'Durlston is quiet and the sea shimmers and you've got the chance of seeing a dolphin'

OLIVIA

Spot dolphins at Durlston

In 1823, William Morton Pitt, MP for Dorset, conceived the idea of turning the small fishing port now known as Swanage into a seaside resort to rival already flourishing Weymouth and Lyme Regis. Local builders took his cue and the coming of the railway in 1885 brought hordes of visitors. The steam train from Norden is still the most stylish way to arrive (see page 20).

One of the developers was George Burt, nephew of John Mowlem who ran a successful and now famous construction firm in London. Between them they built a pier, improved the roads and sewers, and provided proper lighting through a new gasworks. Victorian lamp posts were shipped from London to adorn the town, as were bollards from the city's streets. They provided useful ballast to prevent ships capsizing on their journey back to Swanage having transported quarried Purbeck stone to the capital. Swanage thus earned the name Little London by the Sea.

George Burt had other, more ambitious, ideas. In 1862 he bought the Durlston estate: more than 100 hectares of unspoilt coastland. He hoped to develop it into a suburb of Swanage, and drew up elaborate plans to build houses, shops and a church, but luckily that never happened. Durlston Country Park is now a designated Site of Special Scientific Interest, a National Nature Reserve, a Special Area of Conservation and part of the Jurassic Coast World Heritage Site.

Self-guided trails lead you through wild-flower meadows, coastal fields (or wares), ancient woodland and, perhaps most spectacularly, along the cliffs. There greater horseshoe bats now roost in old stone quarries called the Tilly Whim Caves (Tilly possibly after a former quarryman, whim after the wooden crane that in the 19th and 20th centuries used to lower the limestone on to the boats below). The cliffs and ledges are nesting grounds for guillemots, razorbills, puffins and fulmars, and there's also a lookout point for dolphins. In April, May, October and November especially, Durlston is one of the best places on the south coast for spotting them; bring a pair of binoculars and look for giveaway signs of white water, circling seabirds and black fins.

Wordsworth's wise saying 'Let nature be your teacher' is one of the many philosophical and scientific inscriptions on and around the chunky Great Globe further east. With Durlston Castle (never a castle but a purpose-built restaurant), it was the centrepiece of Burt's grand plans. Some 3 metres in diameter, it's made from Portland stone and weighs an astronomical 40 tonnes.

BH19 2JL

OS SZ032773

AMPLE PARKING (PAY AND DISPLAY)

TOILETS WITH DISABLED ACCESS AND BABY-CHANGING FACILITIES

WELCOME ON LEADS

SEVENTHWAVE CAFÉ, OPEN DAILY 9.30AM–4.30PM (☎ 01929 421111)

SWANAGE

'Kingcombe's really peaceful and there's lots of wild flowers, grasshoppers and butterflies.'
TOBY

Tiptoe through the fields at Kingcombe

When John Walbridge, the tenant of Lower Kingcombe in the valley of the River Hooke, bought 180 hectares of land from the Earl of Sandwich in 1918, it was described as 'a famous dairy farm noted for its Dorset Blue cheese and butter'. Dorset butter was highly regarded in London where it fetched a premium price, but making it left farmers with large quantities of skimmed milk which they turned into a hard, veiny cheese called Dorset Blue Vinny. It was Thomas Hardy's favourite.

Under John Walbridge's stewardship, followed by his son Arthur, the ancient hedgerows, fields and hay meadows at Kingcombe retained their wholeness and integrity, unsprayed by chemicals and untouched by artificial fertilisers of the 20th century. But after Arthur's death in 1985, the entire estate, which had been first mentioned in the Domesday Book, was bought by a London property speculator, broken up into lots and put out to auction. There was public outcry and the Dorset Wildlife Trust successfully purchased 'the farm that time forgot'.

A visit to Kingcombe is a step back to another age. It's still managed as a working farm, grazed by cows and sheep, without any recourse to modern agricultural methods. There are green lanes unchanged since medieval times, and many of the fields have kept their centuries-old names – some, such as Washington's Common, Whittles Common and Keech's Common, called after early owners or tenants. All the habitats are rich in wild flowers, insects, butterflies and birds: in 2010 the BBC filmed *Springwatch* there.

Time moves slowly in parts of Dorset. In 1939 there was only one tractor in Toller Porcorum: virtually all the ploughing was still done by horses. Electricity didn't reach the village until the year before, when Wessex Electric offered three lights and a plug to anyone who wanted them. Just down the road is Powerstock Common, variously known as Poorwood and Poorstock, claimed as a royal hunting ground by King John in the 13th century. It's skirted by the now-defunct railway line that once ran between Maiden Newton and Bridport, depositing holidaymakers at West Bay (see page 17). In spring and summer there are wild flowers galore in the old cutting and in the ancient woods you may just catch sight of a primeval beast. Toller Porcorum means 'valley of the pigs' and the escape of some wild boar from a local farm a few years ago has resulted in their return to the Dorset countryside.

TOLLER PORCORUM

DT2 OEQ

OS SY554980

AMPLE FREE PARKING

TOILETS WITH DISABLED ACCESS

WELCOME ON LEADS

THE KINGCOMBE CAFÉ,
OPEN FRIDAY TO SUNDAY
MARCH TO OCTOBER,
11AM–4.30PM
(☎ 01300 320684)

MAN O'WAR BAY

'The best bit was running up and down the paths. The water was as blue as a swimming pool' MATT

Get in the mood at the Blue Pool

In 1911, Augustus John, one of the greatest portrait artists of his generation, started work on *The Blue Pool*, a study of a striking dark-haired woman reclining in what might be a sun-drenched Mediterranean landscape. The setting isn't the south of France, though, but Furzebrook in Dorset: the Blue Pool, which officially opened to the public with the building of a tea room in 1935, was one of the county's first visitor attractions and is still one of its most enigmatic.

Early tourists flocked to marvel at the chameleon nature of the water, constantly changing in colour from aqua to green to turquoise to ochre with every hue in between. The reason for this phenomenon is to do with clay: fine particles suspended in the pool, which is up to 12 metres deep, diffract light in different ways depending on the ambient temperature. For the Blue Pool was once a clay quarry, the centre of an important industry that continues in the area to this day.

Though the Romans carried out clay mining of some sort in and around Wareham, it has only occurred on a large scale since the late 16th century. At that time the local ball clay was found to be particularly suitable for the manufacture of tobacco pipes and, later, when the drinking of tea and coffee became fashionable in the 18th century, for fine tableware. In 1791 the owners of the Furzebrook estate signed a contract with a young potter named Josiah Wedgwood to supply regular shipments of high-grade clay for his Staffordshire works (the order still stands).

The legacy of all this activity remains in the rainwater-filled Blue Pool, now a designated Site of Special Scientific Interest because of the rare wildlife within its surrounding hectares of heath, woodland and gorse. Sandy paths lead down to small white beaches on the water's edge, up to heady views of the Purbeck Hills, or out through lofty pine trees for glimpses of the lake. Reward yourself afterwards with home-baked scones in the original wood-floored tea room.

The town of Wareham itself is also well worth a visit. Walk round the 9th-century walls, including Bloody Bank where five local rebels were executed by order of Judge Jeffreys after the Monmouth Rebellion (see page 25), or hire a rowing boat or canoe at the historic quay on the River Frome. If there on the second weekend in December, keep a lookout for Father Christmas who every year climbs down the chimney of the Red Lion hotel at the Cross before handing out presents to local children. His mode of transport is always different: in 2000 he arrived by camel.

WAREHAM

	BH20 5AR
OS	SY935832
P	PARKING INCLUDED IN TICKET PRICE

| | TOILETS WITH DISABLED ACCESS AND BABY-CHANGING FACILITIES |
| | WELCOME ON LEADS |

| | BLUE POOL TEAHOUSE, OPEN DAILY (WINTER EXCEPTED) FROM 10AM (☎ 01929 551408) |

'I liked the hide because you could see all the birds and deer so clearly.' MARK

Track down deer at Arne

The Arne peninsula is a place of contradictions. On the one hand, it feels remote enough to be the edge of the world; on the other, it's almost cheek by jowl with the densely populated town of Poole (see page 51). But that strange juxtaposition doesn't seem to bother the wildlife. Arne is one of the RSPB's oldest reserves, with flat, sandy paths suitable for kids (though not so good for buggies), and a great place to get up close to nature.

The backcloth to Arne is lowland heathland, an internationally rare habitat. It was created by prehistoric settlers who started felling forests to grow crops for food and to encourage grass for domestic animals. Where the soils were poor, heather and gorse began to dominate the cleared landscape. Heathland provided not only grazing for cattle, ponies, pigs and sheep, but bracken for bedding, compost and fuel. Tall heather was used for thatching, flowering heather for beer and honey, and ling, broom and birch were used to make besoms (witches' brooms).

From the 18th century, however, heaths were converted to farmland and built on as towns expanded. Now only a third remains of the UK's 1,500 square kilometres of lowland heathland – 11 per cent of it in Dorset. Visit Arne in spring or summer, when the heath is ablaze with sweet-scented yellow gorse, followed by the pink and purple haze of heather. In winter, the landscape turns stark and brown, while flocks of waders and wildfowl swirl across the shallow waters of Poole harbour. Herds of sika deer can be seen all year round. Catch sight of them sheltering in wooded areas, or spy on them at close quarters from one of the hides.

The fields at the centre of the reserve, just off the main track to Shipstal Point where there's a narrow beach and stunning views across the harbour, are alive with linnet, goldfinch and chaf-finch in summer and flocks of redwing, fieldfare and starling in winter. On sunny days watch out for basking reptiles: Arne is home to all six British species (see page 71), including the rare smooth snake (named after its flat, ridgeless scales) and the adder, the only venomous snake in much of northern Europe. It used to be believed that crossing the path of an adder would bring bad luck, and in Dorset even now an adder appearing on a doorstep is said to mean someone in the house-hold is sure to die. At Arne just bear in mind Spike Milligan's words, 'There's nothing madder than a trodden-on adder', and give them a respectful berth.

BH20 5BJ

OS SY971876

PAY AND DISPLAY CAR PARK

TOILETS WITH DISABLED ACCESS AND BABY-CHANGING FACILITIES

WELCOME ON LEADS

THE ARNE CAFÉ, OPEN DAILY 9.30AM–4.30PM (01929 553360)

WAREHAM

PUNCH & JUDY

'I like going to Weymouth Beach and paddling in the sea because it cools you down'
EMMA

Be beside the seaside in Weymouth

The bustling town of Weymouth (named Budmouth by Thomas Hardy) began life in the 12th century as two separate medieval ports on either side of the mouth of the River Wey. Weymouth was on the south, Melcombe Regis on the north; and it was through Melcombe Regis that the Black Death probably came to England in 1348. In 1571 the two towns were united and, from 1760, grew hugely fashionable as a resort where visitors could try out sea-bathing. A local medic, Dr Crane, who recommended the drinking of sea water for health purposes, was loud in his praise: 'The Sea-Water of this fine Bay is quite pure, of a beautiful azure Colour, perfectly clear and transparent; the Sands under Foot are soft, yet firm: entirely clear and free from Sea-Weeds, Rocks, Slippery Stones or any Kind of Obstruction whatever. The Declivity is so gradual as to be almost imperceptible; a great Security to the weak and fearful.'

All the above remains true of Weymouth Beach today, and for a traditional bucket-and-spade day out beside the sea it can hardly be bettered (Lyme Regis, to the west, and Swanage, to the east, are close contenders). Apart from the obvious abundance of ice cream, candyfloss and fish and chips, there are pedaloes for hire, Punch and Judy shows and old-fashioned donkey rides. Weymouth is also home to the award-winning sand sculptor Mark Anderson.

Watching over the proceedings is an imposing stone statue of King George III, who holidayed in the town nearly every summer from 1789 to 1805, doing wonders for its popularity. When he entered the sea a band played 'God Save the King' from the bathing machine behind him. There was no free swimming or even paddling in those days – horse-drawn huts on wheels afforded safety and privacy. Immersion was carefully timed, and female bathers voluminously clad. It's King George III, too, riding the Osmington Horse, a chalk hill figure about 4 miles north-east of Weymouth. By all accounts, the king was none too pleased with the artwork as it showed him riding away from, rather than into, the town.

If you're in Weymouth in the month of May, don't miss the annual international kite festival on the beach (see page 27). The town's historic harbour is also well worth a visit. A two-minute ride on a rowing-boat ferry will take you from the northern quayside to the Nothe Gardens and Victorian fort, whose warren of accessible tunnels is believed to be haunted.

WEYMOUTH

🅿 DT4 7SX

OS SY686810

🅿 AMPLE PARKING (PAY AND DISPLAY)

♿ PUBLIC TOILETS WITH DISABLED ACCESS

🚫 NOT PERMITTED ON MAIN BEACH EASTER TO END OCTOBER

🏛 THE STABLE, CUSTOM HOUSE QUAY, OPEN DAILY FROM 5PM (☎ 01305 789389)

'The reeds at Radipole are very beautiful and many birds nest there' JONATHAN

Watch the birds at Radipole

Five minutes from the centre of Weymouth, easily accessible on foot from the beach (see page 83), is Radipole Lake, created in 1872 when a dam was built across the mouth of the River Wey. It had long been renowned for its rare and important wildlife, with the Earl of Ilchester donating a herd of swans and a swanherd: an island was built in the estuary for the purpose.

In 1929 the area was declared a bird sanctuary by the borough council and the rest, as they say, is history. Now well-surfaced paths and wooden boardwalks weave round the lake through one of the largest reedbeds in south-west England. Reedbeds were traditionally grown as cover for duck shoots and to protect mudflats from tidal erosion, but their main use was for thatch, once the most common roofing material in Dorset. With the decline in thatching, they are now one of the UK's rarest habitats – up to 40 per cent were lost between 1949 and 1990.

Radipole is bird heaven. In spring you may catch sight of a sedge warbler as it pirouettes up from the tops of bushes singing its scratchy song, or you may hear the pinging calls of a bearded tit as it flashes through the waving reeds. The reserve has several breeding pairs of great crested grebe, whose tiny, stripy chicks can be seen riding on their parents' backs. The summer plumage of great crested grebes was once so fashionable in the hat-making industry that the species was almost extinct by 1860. This cruel persecution led to the formation of the RSPB, which now runs the reserves at Radipole and nearby Lodmoor.

Other stars of Radipole include bitterns, whose booming song sounds like someone blowing gently over the top of a milk bottle, and marsh harriers, now breeding again in Dorset for the first time in 50 years. Sit quietly in the North Hide and observe electric-blue kingfishers nesting or feeding, or use the RSPB telescope to watch dapper tufted ducks diving underwater as they put on a show in front of the panoramic viewing window in the thatched visitor centre.

There you can also borrow a kids' activity backpack and binoculars from the friendly and knowledgeable staff, or pick up a copy of bird bingo, which gets the whole family searching for birds, bugs, butterflies, flowers and rarities like otters and water voles. Nets are available for pond-dipping, as is seed for duck-feeding. If you spend just a couple of hours here, you'll feel your stress levels drop dramatically. Remarkably, entry is free though donations are always welcome.

	WEYMOUTH

- DT4 7TZ
- **OS** SY675795
- **P** HUGE NEARBY CAR PARK (PAY AND DISPLAY)
- TOILETS WITH DISABLED ACCESS AND BABY-CHANGING FACILITIES
- WELCOME ON LEADS
- RADIPOLE LAKE CAFÉ, OPEN DAILY 9AM–4PM (☎ 01305 778313)

'You feel like a giant in Wimborne's model village'.

FIONA

Travel back in time at Wimborne Minster

Of all the smugglers who operated along the Dorset coast in the 18th and 19th centuries, Isaac Gulliver is by far the most notorious. By the time he died in 1822, he had amassed great wealth and was the owner of several farms and houses with numerous hiding places for goods such as brandy, gin, tea, tobacco, sugar, lace and silks. Once, when the customs men were on their way to arrest him, he famously pretended to be a corpse, powdering his face to a deathly white and lying lifeless in a coffin. Then, in an extraordinary conversion, the man who'd been the scourge of the authorities retired to Wimborne and became a pillar of the community. He ended his days as one of the church wardens of the minster after which the town is named.

There's a memorial to Gulliver in the minster, the only twin-towered church in Dorset. The 12th-century central tower used to support a tall spire until, one day during a service in 1600, it came crashing to the ground, luckily avoiding injury to the congregation. On the outside, high up in the west tower, facing out over the green, is a charming Quarter Jack – a miniature soldier in 19th-century uniform who strikes the hours and quarters throughout the day. Inside the minster there's an extraordinarily complicated astronomical clock, which not only tells the time with a 24-hour dial but also marks the phases of the moon. Upstairs, above the vestry, is one of the UK's oldest chained libraries, founded in 1686 not just for the use of the clergy but also for the 'shopkeepers and better class of person of Wimborne'. There are about 400 volumes, all leather bound and the majority still fastened together, as was the norm at a time when a single edition could equal the price of a farm.

One of the oldest buildings in Wimborne is the Priest's House, now an imaginative museum. Themed displays, including a Georgian parlour and a working Victorian kitchen, bring home what life was like in east Dorset through the centuries. The high point is the 17th-century hall laid out as a Victorian schoolroom, complete with hard old benches and squeaky chalk boards. Get your little darlings to practise their handwriting by copying out homilies such as 'Honour thy father and mother', sit up straight with their shoulders back, chest out and head up, or stand in the corner wearing the dunce's cap. Of course they may turn the tables on you by donning the costume provided to become a cane-brandishing Victorian teacher!

WIMBORNE

🏠 BH21 1HR
OS SU010000
🅿 PUBLIC CAR PARK ON KING STREET

♿ TOILETS WITH DISABLED ACCESS AND BABY-CHANGING FACILITIES
🐕 ASSISTANCE DOGS ONLY

🍽 GARDEN TEA ROOM, PRIEST'S HOUSE MUSEUM, OPEN MONDAY TO SATURDAY 10AM–4PM
(☎ 01202 882533)

'I really liked the colourful tented room. It reminded me of a circus big top.' LORNA

Ogle an obelisk at Kingston Lacy

In the middle of the lawn behind the 17th-century mansion of Kingston Lacy there's a surprising sight. Standing 6 metres high, the Philae Needle is an ancient Egyptian obelisk brought back from the banks of the Nile by the eccentric former owner of the big house, William John Bankes. He first spotted it while abroad in 1815 but it wasn't installed at the family home until 1839, when it took a team of 19 horses to haul it upright. Nearby is a stone sarcophagus given to William by the British consul, who in 1822 wrote hoping it would 'form an acceptable addition to your Egyptian antiquities'. Kingston Lacy has the largest private collection of such artefacts in the UK. Many are on display in the house.

William was unstoppable. With the help of Sir Charles Barry, architect of the Houses of Parliament, he transformed Kingston Lacy into an Italianate palazzo, filled with pictures and other works of art acquired on his extensive travels: paintings by Rubens, Van Dyck, Titian and Tintoretto, tulip vases from the 1600s when a single tulip could cost thousands of pounds, elaborate torchères (lights) with gold tortoise-shaped feet and even a grand marble staircase bought in Italy. The *pièce de résistance* was the Spanish Room, whose walls are lined with Venetian leather and which positively glitters with gold. Kids will love the guest bedrooms at the top of the house, draped from ceiling height with heavy fabric to look like tents.

The Bankes family were an unusual lot. On the stairs is a bronze statue of Brave Dame Mary, holding the 31 keys of Corfe Castle which she twice defended in the Civil War (see page 21). One of her descendants, John Bankes the Younger, earned the reputation of a miser, always wearing a long dressing gown to save the expense of trousers. Henrietta Bankes, who ran the estate in the early 20th century, laid out the formal and sunken gardens. 'The park and the garden were meticulously tended,' recalled Henrietta's daughter Viola. 'To Daphne, Ralph and me, not even realising how lucky we were, as long as we obeyed the rules, it was a perfectly ordered Paradise.'

Under the care of the National Trust, that's still the case today. There are woodland walks through the vast landscaped park which is grazed by a herd of Red Devon cattle, and endless outdoor areas to explore, including a Japanese tea garden and a walled kitchen garden where there are chickens and pigs as well as wheelbarrows and watering cans for green-fingered kids.

WIMBORNE

⊞ BH21 4EA

OS ST976012

🚻 TOILETS WITH BABY-CHANGING FACILITIES

🅿 AMPLE FREE PARKING

🐾 WELCOME ON SHORT LEADS IN PARK AND WOODLAND

🍴 KINGSTON LACY RESTAURANT, OPEN DAILY 10AM–4PM (☎ 01202 883402)

'I really loved watching the monkeys playing' LAURA

Monkey around at Monkey World

In the eleventh book of Lemony Snicket's *A Series of Unfortunate Events*, it is said that having a personal philosophy is like owning a pet marmoset: 'It may be very attractive when you acquire it, but there may be situations when it will not come in handy at all.' Jim Cronin, who in 1987 started transforming a disused Dorset pig farm into a rescue centre for apes and monkeys, wouldn't have agreed. Monkey World is now a 26-hectare wildlife park that's home to more than 240 primates of 16 different species. It works with governments worldwide to halt the illegal smuggling of apes and monkeys from Africa, Asia and South America; it's even had its own TV series.

Monkey World is not a zoo and the primates are not exhibits. Many have been rescued from laboratories and circuses, others from use as beach-photographers' props. The enclosures give the animals some semblance of living in the wild. Telephone poles, recycled plastic lumber and fire hoses have all come in handy to build complex climbing frames with hammocks, swings, bridges and multi-level walkways. Blankets, sheets and towels provide ideal nesting material: chimpanzees and orangutans make new beds to sleep in every night.

The similarity between orangutans and humans is uncanny. Both species are great apes, with large brains, forward-facing eyes and gripping hands. Pregnancy in female orangutans lasts for about eight and a half months and the young stay with their mothers until they're about seven or eight years old – longer than any other primate apart from *Homo sapiens*. Chimpanzees are even closer to us in their genetic make-up. Probably the most intelligent non-human animal, they demonstrate learned behaviours, long memories and extraordinary use of tools.

In the orangutan crèche at Monkey World, you can get face to face with these distant relatives of ours, separated only by a thick pane of glass. The fascination seems to work both ways, with the orangutans mirroring the behaviour of human visitors. Elsewhere, there are viewing platforms so that you can look down into enclosures as the woolly monkeys and gibbons show off their acrobatics, and a walk-through area where the ring-tailed lemurs from Madagascar roam freely.

When your little monkeys have had enough, they can let off steam on human swings and climbing frames in the Great Ape Play Area. Don't miss the Chilean monkey puzzle tree, so called because someone in the early 19th century remarked: 'To climb that would puzzle a monkey.'

WOOL

🚾 BH20 6HH
OS SY847885
🅿 AMPLE FREE PARKING

♿ TOILETS WITH DISABLED ACCESS AND BABY-CHANGING FACILITIES
🐕 ASSISTANCE DOGS ONLY

☕ TREETOPS CAFÉ, OPEN DAILY 10AM–5PM (☎ 01929 462537)

'I liked the dressing up and
I liked the trenches because
it felt real' GABRIELLE

Ride in a tank at Bovington

When T.E. Lawrence (see page 49) first came to Bovington Camp in 1923, it was just a muddy street with a hotchpotch of shops and cafés known as Tintown, while the troops were put up in wooden huts. Seeking anonymity, he'd joined the Tank Corps under the name of Private T.E. Shaw and was known as Broughy Shaw because of his beloved Brough motorcycle.

Tanks had started arriving in Dorset in 1916, and within two years Bovington was the main training centre for Tank Corps personnel. It's now famous for its tank museum, a collection of more than 250 tanks and armoured fighting vehicles from across the world. Here you can feel the ground shake as up to 60 tonnes of heavy metal roll into action in the outdoor arena, and you can also thunder around in a specially converted tracked vehicle.

Displays in six vast hangars explain why tanks were invented – to break the stalemate of the First World War when machine-gun fire, mud and barbed wire made movement impossible across the miles of trenches on the Western Front. Leonardo da Vinci had designed an early example in the 1480s, but the first tank ever made, Little Willie, didn't appear on the battlefield until 1916. With a top speed of 3 mph, and needing to stop to fire its gun, it was a world away from modern machines which can go up to 40 mph and still fire accurately on the move.

In no way does the tank museum glorify war. 'My closing memories are that tank-fighting was the most horrific form of land fighting in the war,' says a British tank commander from the Second World War. The trench experience takes visitors from the First World War recruiting office, where soldiers were weighed and measured, through arrival at Calais station, with crates piled high and the wounded lying groaning on stretchers, to the ultimate destination at the Front. It's impossible to convey the full horror of it all, but at Bovington they give it a good try.

Elsewhere you can design a tank, dress up in combat gear, fire machine guns and peer inside a cross-section of Challenger 2, the modern British Army's main battle tank, crewed by four. The overwhelming impression is one of discomfort: you can be shut inside for days at a time, and it's dark, hot, cramped and smelly. You can't get up and move around, you can't stretch out or lie down, and you dare not open a hatch or climb outside. There's a heater that can be used to cook packeted food, but nowhere to go to the loo: just a tube. And not a moment's privacy.

WOOL

BH20 6JG

OS SY831884

P AMPLE FREE PARKING

TOILETS WITH DISABLED ACCESS AND BABY-CHANGING FACILITIES

ASSISTANCE DOGS ONLY

THE TANK MUSEUM RESTAURANT, OPEN DAILY 10AM–4.30PM (☎ 01929 405096)

'The view from the caves was amazing. It was fun skimming stones across the rocks into the water' JOEY

Feel the force in Winspit Caves

It could be a scene from *Harry Potter*: a series of echoey chasms with the sea lashing at the cliffs just metres away. No surprise to hear that Winspit, an abandoned quarry near Worth Matravers on the Isle of Purbeck, has in the past been used for filming episodes of *Doctor Who*.

Purbeck stone in all its types has been sought after by masons, sculptors and builders since Roman times. The villages of Worth and Langton Matravers, as well as nearby Corfe Castle, were built from it, and in the 19th century it was shipped from Swanage to pave the streets of London (see page 73). Decorative Purbeck 'marble' – actually a limestone composed of millions of fresh-water snails – embellishes English medieval cathedrals such as Westminster, Durham, Salisbury and York. But it had a price. Conditions underground were cramped, dirty and dangerous. Boys as young as 10 toiled alongside men quarrying the stone from tunnels less than a metre high.

In the Second World War, Winspit and neighbouring Seacombe quarries, neither of which had been worked since the 1900s, were employed for naval and air defence; at that time, too, the village of Worth Matravers became a top-secret centre for radar research, with huge towers and military buildings marching across the fields, though you'd never know it today. Now the caves are home to quieter occupants: rare greater horseshoe bats which are protected under law.

Climb back up the hill and reward yourself with a drink at the historic Square and Compass inn, which also has a small fossil museum. Dinosaurs were demonstrably present in the area 140 million years ago: a series of 52 hefty footprints, the tracks of around a dozen sauropods, were found in a nearby quarry in 1997. Buried in Worth Matravers churchyard is local farmer Benjamin Jesty, who in 1774 used a steel knitting needle and pus from a cow's udder to inoculate his wife and two children against smallpox. Remarkably, the experiment worked, beating the physician Edward Jenner by 20 years.

If you've been inspired by your visit to Winspit, you might want to stop off at the Burngate Stone Carving Centre, just outside Langton Matravers, which runs courses and taster sessions for all ages. Or you might be feeling adventurous, in which case follow the path out from Langton Matravers to Dancing Ledge (possibly so called because it's the size of a ballroom floor), where a swimming pool was blasted into the rock for local schools at the beginning of the 20th century.

BH19 3LF

OS SY977760

FREE PUBLIC CAR PARK (DONATION BOX)

PUBLIC TOILETS IN THE CAR PARK

WELCOME, BUT BE CAREFUL ON THE CLIFFS

THE SQUARE AND COMPASS, OPEN DAILY FROM 12PM
(☎ 01929 439229)

WORTH MATRAVERS

For Bee, Emily, Joey and Nicky

ACKNOWLEDGEMENTS

Grateful thanks to the children and staff at St Osmund's Middle School and Sherborne Primary School, who shared their favourite Dorset activities with me and helped get the book started. To all those who accompanied me on visits or gave me quotes and suggestions, including Mac Allen, Emma Andre, Isabel Andre, Mark Andre, Tina Andre, Eadie Ayres, Alex Cocker, Maddy Cregg, Olivia Cregg, Anneka Dawkins, David Dawkins, Heidi Flint, Bee Forder, Emma Goldman, Harriet Goldman-Thompson, Chris Harris, Laura Harrold, Susie Kibuga, Rebecca Longman, Joey Moxon, Nicky Moxon, Martha Oakes, Amber Rushall, Emily Rushall, Rowan Seymour, Lorna Simpson, Andrew Wood and Stella Wood. To Julie and Tim Musk for believing in the idea, and to Daniel Rushall for his inspirational photographs and Emily Moxon for her stylish design. To Matilda Richards for picking up the ball and running with it. To Blandford Fashion Museum, Dorset County Museum and Poole Museum for permission to take pictures on their premises. To Mandy Cooper of Dorset Cereals and Katie Burt of Positive PR for enthusiasm and advice. And to my parents, Mike and Jane Forder, for bringing me to Dorset in the first place.